TRUE HEARTH

TRUE HEARTH

A Practical Guide to Traditional Householding

by

James Allen Chisholm

Elder, Ring of Troth

Second
Improved Edition

RÛNA-RAVEN PRESS

Second Improved Edition, 1994

Published by
RUNA-RAVEN PRESS
P.O. Box 557
Smithville, Texas 78957

Printed in the United States of America

Introduction

This is a book about the true Teutonic household. It is about living in a sacred way in tune with the spiritual values of our ancestors. These ancestral ways we call the *true* ways, or ways *loyal* to the elder troth. The true household has a strength and vitality not available in most contemporary households. The hearts of the folk in a true household are firmly rooted in the rich earth of their heritage, and tap into the spiritual power (haming) of their ancestors. The folk then can manifest and wield these almost forgotten and languishing forces.

In the days of yore the family or clan was the basic social unit-- it was a survival team. Being true to the ways of our heritage can bring the power and joy of the ancient Teutonic household alive today. Ward our household well with the might of our holy gods and ancestors. Whether our household is made up of a single family, or a multiplicity of individuals and families who have come together as a tribe, or even composed of a single individual, the folkish ways of the troth will give your home a warmth and magic unlike any other.

A strong household is a good antidote to the alienation that results in so many of our social ills-- including rampant drug and alcohol problems and even many of our economic woes. Members of a true family can act as individuals, but they will have the strength of the household behind them, and the household will have their strength in times of need.

At heart many of your values and ways may be truer and more heathen than you might think now. This book will make it possible for you to be aware of how true you have been all along and to be so in a more conscious manner. You will be provided with a body of traditional Teutonic household lore that may at first seem quite "new." Many of the customs you practice in celebrating Easter, Yule-tide ("Christmas") and other holidays are entirely Teutonic and heathen. So rejoice! Rejoice and know that the fires of truth, the fires of our ancestral ways never died. Our people never really completely abandoned the elder troth. The fading embers of our troth burn yet, and their fires may burn brightly in our hearts again-- if we only feed them with the breath of our lives and the kindling of our efforts.

It was into the household the heathen ways retreated under suppression, it is in the household they live on in hiding, and it is from the household the shall spring forth again in all their glory.

Part I
Holy Powers

Chapter 2
THE FOREFATHERS AND FOREMOTHERS

The heart of the household is its folk, and this is the heart of household religion. The folk of the household may be comprised of a clan made up of a nuclear family or people from different families who choose to live together as a family or tribe. The Troth is not only a religion practiced by our ancestors— it is also practiced in honor of them.

We are all probably familiar with the symbol of the so-called family tree. The origin of this conception lies deep in the roots of or folk memories. European folk have generally thought the world, and the generations of things of all kinds to be somehow in the form of a *tree*. That is, things are generated from a root which is deep in the dark recesses of the past, rise to a point (or a line) in the present "trunk" of the here and now, and branch out into the youngest levels of existence trailing off into the "yet to be." The dead ancestors are the roots of the tree, we the living are the trunk, and the branches are the young children (who are the ancestors reborn) and the leaves of the next spring are the descendants yet to be born. All of this is an organic *whole*. In other words, the dead are as much a part of the family as the living, and the yet unborn are equal to the dead— because they essentially *are* the dead reborn.

Memories of ancestors are sacred. The might of our forebears' deeds are brought to life regularly and made manifest in our hearts and minds when we think of them. We do this in holy times and places. There we have greater access to their spiritual power. The stories of ancestral deeds remind us of clanic values and virtues— of the most important and core characteristics of our clanic and tribal heritage. In the deeds of our forebears we may find models for effective action especially well suited to our own temperaments.

Knowledge of our forebears is a very special form of our-*selves*— at least it is for those deep in knowledge of the lore. It is easier to objectify our own behavior when we see it in another. Reflection on the workings of a kindred soul can offer us deep understanding of ourselves and the world. Likewise we may think on the works wrought by our folk when acting collectively at the tribal or national level to know the tribal or folk soul(s) that shape the lives of our societies and communities.

Among those we honor as our forefolk we may number historical and mythic figures from the past for whom we feel an affinity or admire, but to whom we are unable to document a line of descent. Unfortunately, and thanks to a thousand to fifteen hundred years of the methodical undoing of our ancestral ways, few of us can document our heritage back to the pre-Christian times, let alone back to first century figures such as Veleda or Arminius. Nevertheless, we may have good reasons to suspect or claim kinship with them and rightly honor them as ancestors in our household workings. On a tribal level we may all be justified in calling such figures ancestors. In Iceland, where the grip of the Church was fairly weak, it is not uncommon for folks to be able to trace their ancestry back to saga figures of the Viking Age.

Some of the folks we may choose to honor as, or along with, our own ancestors may include heroes from myth and history. Mythic figures may remind us of valued or important qualities of our families, or of the ideals for which we strive. From accounts of mythologized heroes such as Ragnar Lodbrok, Sigurd Fafnir's Bane, Hervor, Starkad, Hadding, Hrolf Kraki, and others we may find models for certain spiritual qualities abstracted and exaggerated in the mythic accounts. In honoring historical figures we may study their actual methods and tactics in real and specific situations as well.

Such heroes my be honored by readings and retellings of their deeds, especially in a working or ritual context. Some, such as Sigurd, may even be honored on film or stage. Attending productions of Richard Wagner's *Ring des Nibelungen* or watching Fritz Lang's production of the *Nibelungenlied* may serve as occasions to honor Sigurd's memory.

Respect for our forefolk may be expressed in a variety of ways. Especially in the way we live our everyday lives. A good life brings honor and luck to the family and ancestors as much as their great works make us strong. Knowledge of their works strengthens our souls to help us do great deeds and thereby increase the power within ourselves and within our clans.

Photos and mementos may be kept and displayed to keep memories of our forefolk alive. In fact, it is not at all uncommon to devote some corner or room of the house to a small shrine in which photo albums are kept. In this shrine objects once owned by the deceased, or other things which serve as mementos and may contain clanic or tribal haming, may be displayed. People whose families have no interest in outward displays of their troth, or are even downright hostile to it, may still experience a ritual reconnection with ancestral power simply by going through photo albums and slide shows in the company of their families. You may notice that as you progress from the latest to the oldest and most venerable of the photos and mementos, the sense of awe and reverence increases.

When toasts to the memory and honor of the forefolks are made these power objects may be brought out to the main harrow, if the family shrine is not a part of the main harrow. This drinking in memory and honor of the ancestors is referred to as drinking to their memory, or "myne." The deeds of some ancestors may be so great that they are worthy of special days of remembrance and memory-drinkings by themselves.

If your family is opposed to the ways of the elder Troth (on a conscious level) you can still honor the ancestors with them without necessarily bringing in the elder Gods and Goddesses. At big family gatherings encourage old people to tell you about their past and what they remember about kin who lived before them. Encourage them to write down as much of it as they

Chapter 3
THE WAYS OF THE ÆSIR AND VANIR

At first glance, the tales of the elder Gods that have come down to us may seem suitable for entertainment, while their spiritual values might elude us. To many the northern mythology holds an incomparable and compelling beauty that is unmatched by that of any of the currently established religions in our society. But deeper understandings are necessary to incorporate the myths into daily life experience in a meaningful way. Such understanding is also needed for the basic forms of religious observation including ways of worship (giving honor to something) and blessing (giving and receiving gifts between the human and divine worlds). Understanding is really won not by belief but by living action. Attending blessings or performing them yourself are ways of bringing the religion alive. Other ways include meditations on the Eddic myths and the sagas and other mythic tales of Germanic folk such as *Bêowulf* or the *Nibelungenlied.*

Understanding of the myths is hindered by the notion that they are valuable only as entertainment — especially for children — and by the fact that they are presented as the silly superstitions of a flock of ignorant savages. The very idea that profound wisdom is contained in the tales of the Germanic Gods and Goddesses has been made to seem preposterous by our cultural biases. The difficulty of understanding the myths is increased by the fact that our contemporary society is so very different from the Viking Age culture from which many of the stories stem.

In the Ring of Troth there is no such thing as a "heretic." There is no set of orthodox dogmas or doctrines to which one must adhere in order to be thought to be *true* (loyal) to the Gods and ancestors. Anyone who professes to be true and attends blessings may be said to be true. It is the birthright of all who are descended from the northern Gods. Legislating belief and imposing it by force is to attempt to tyrannize and control the deepest thoughts and feelings, the very souls, the spirituality of a people. Uniform belief is not possible without uniform experience and mental machinery. This is neither desirable nor possible. On some levels we all share in our understanding of the Gods and Goddesses— while on other levels we are likely to differ widely.

One question that arises first is just who or what are the Gods anyway? There are many ways of answering this question and all of them are correct on some level for some people. There are two factors to consider in seeking an answer to this inquiry. The first thing to consider is whether an idea *rings true*— whether you can intuitively relate it to your own experience, spiritual or otherwise. The other thing you might consider is whether it is *traditional* or not. This means that solid basis for the belief can be found in the record of past beliefs and practices of the folk in question. It is useless to invoke the traditions of "Atlantis" or "Thule," or any other subjective creation in this regard. There is no *traditional* basis for these beliefs.

In any event, personal experience should always be the deciding factor for adhering to a theological premise which is of little value if it is not real to you. If a certain view of the Gods seems to ring true to your previous experiences with the holy and with life then it will more likely be *real*ized in your soul— and it will work for you all the better. If it works for you, it is true on a basic level.

The Teutonic tradition is one that values change and flux. It is also common for true folk to change their views of the Gods and Goddesses as their knowledge of the lore deepens and is brought together with their life experiences. What is real at one time, and for one level of being, may not work at another time or level.

Generally people do not radically change their basic understandings of the Gods, but gradually expand their understandings. Radical changes are most likely in those who begin with a highly eclectic or non-Germanic understanding of the religion. In a particularly extreme case someone might at first interpret the Troth in terms of Christian theology and their Christian religious experience. Such persons might at first allow their previous concepts to dominate their thinking. But the more they think about the northern Gods and Goddesses and the more they participate in the northern ways of worship the less the old patterns are likely to fit and truer patterns will rise as revelations from within to take their place. Such a person may slowly discard the Christian patterns of thought, or else reinterpret them entirely in terms of northern spirituality.

Ironically, sometimes those who begin with Christian patterns have an easier time than those who have mastered the folk or philosophical traditions of other exotic cultures. This is because at the folk level Christianity only took hold because it was heavily laden with element from the old folk culture. Little, if any, of the actual official doctrinaire theology of the Church ever seemed to get incorporated into the folk religion. Instead, the Christian mythology and religion were commonly reinterpreted in terms of native folkish ways— Christianity was modified to be in accord with Germanic concepts and practices and so in many instances was made *true*. The Church embarked on a conscious policy of not only allowing, but of encouraging this. Otherwise, folks were simply unable to assimilate Christianity and it make real for themselves. For this reason many of the old Germanic Gods survive as saints and may of our ancient rites survive as folk customs.

There are a number of theologies prevalent among modern heathens. Some are very practical and almost entirely unconcerned with metaphysics. In fact some are not even concerned with the whole matter of what the Gods are like. The simple fact that the Gods and Goddesses *are* is good enough for them. To some, the core essence of the Troth amounts to a system of ethics and values perhaps unconcerned with the Gods. For these folks patterns of behavior might be derived from the sagas, *Bêowulf*, and other works of heroic and historic literature which reflect pre-Christian ways of doing and being. To many of the pragmatists who do concern themselves with theology, the Gods are role models and exemplify behavior appropriate to certain paths of life. Here the Gods and Goddesses may be taken as symbols or examples.

Some might take this to be almost "atheistic," when in fact it is not. The Gods may be acknowledged as *real*, but not reduced to the same level of reality as the strict polytheists would have them.

It is often found that if a pragmatist and a polytheist discuss things long enough they will eventually see themselves as differing as a result of semantics. Both can agree that the Gods have an existence independent of the individual worshippers and that they are eternal. It is just a matter of exactly how they accomplish this. The pragmatist might argue that the Gods exist as a part of the collective cultural consciousness and that this is the source of their life. A strict polytheist might say that the divinities are transcendent living beings made up of a numinous energy and that they live and think much as we do. Some might even say that all the stories of the Gods are literally true. However, most would agree that these events "took place" in some unhistorical realm before time as we know it was in evidence and which extends beyond the realm we now know as temporal. This is a "time" which always was, is *now,* and which will always be. This is the kind of "time" we seek to enter in ritual and in the blessings when we come together with the Gods and Goddesses of our ancestors.

Deity is seen by some in terms of pantheistic magical force that pervades the universe. One concept of this is contained in the Old Norse word *ginn-*, as in the English "be-*ginn*-ing." Before time or space existed there was the *Ginn-unga-gap*: the magically charged void. In it were/are potentially contained all the possibilities of existence and evolution.

There is another understanding of the Gods which needs some discussion. Euhemerism is the belief that the Gods and Goddesses of the folk were actually human men and women of the past who were "immortalized" due to their great feats (of heroism or trickery). This view is historically a sign of decay in the religion— or as often as not it is used as propaganda against heathen faiths. The Danish historian — and cleric — Saxo Grammaticus held that the elder Gods and Goddesses were "magicians" who were overcome by the teachings of the Church.

A form of monotheism is also quite common among true folk. These would have it that either Odin (All-Father) or Tyr is the one true and only God and that all other divine entities are aspects of him. This is probably the clearest form of the influence of Christianity on the attitudes toward the elder divinities.

The Odian view has it that consciousness is a very rare thing in the universe— a gift bestowed upon humanity and some semi-divine wights and that consciousness is the most holy and godly thing in the universe. The

Gods and Goddesses are structures within this substance of consciousness. Odians often see deities in terms of Jungian archetypes. In this contexts it may be said that the stories of the Gods and Goddesses metaphorically express truths about the natural or physical world, the soul, magical initiation, or realities that cannot be expressed with ordinary language at all. Such people hold that the divinities are expressions of ineffable metaphysical and metalinguistic truths. The myths serve as vehicle to express truths in all of these areas of life.

Which of these is being expressed by a given story will depend on who is telling the story. The Eddic sources are usually told from an Odinic or Odian viewpoint. This is so because the poets who composed the poems were almost without exception themselves *Óðinsmenn* — Men of Odin — as Odin is the "patron" of poets and magicians. But other views can be extracted from the material as most of these stories were most likely familiar throughout the ancient culture. Diverse attitudes towards divinity and the Gods existed then— and they inevitably exist now. This is not a *problem*, it is a *solution*.

The spiritual road you travel may have much to do with the path you travel in life and the activities you choose to identify yourself with. For most people this is likely to be based on their professions or trades. In heathen times one's concept of the Gods and the divine had a great deal to do with one's function in society. Different kinds of people had different kinds of Gods— so it was then — so it *really* is today.

The mythology may be interpreted in terms of society, nature and the soul. How an individual tends to interpret the mythology will depend on the area of life in which that individual is most active and concerned. This will depend a great deal on the person's work in the context of society.

The social interpretations are the most universal since all share communally in the life of the society. It is always easy to see some social moral or lesson in the myths, though the interpretations of a single myth can vary enormously depending on who is doing the telling and/or listening.

The social role a person fills will determine the kinds of things he or she sees in society, the kinds of knowledge it is possible for an individual to have about society. Each person will only be familiar with certain spheres of activity and be more or less ignorant of others. This more so nowadays than in the pre-industrial era when the division of labor was less pronounced.

The Gods and Goddesses

In modern terms the Germanic Gods and Goddesses can be classified very generally according to three "functions." The first function is that of *administration*, the second is *military*, and the third is *production*. This scheme is very general, but is highly useful as a tool for understanding the social implications of the myths and Gods and Goddesses in them.

The first function is dually aspected— rulership requires both kings and priests (or magicians). Kings administer law and order in the land— while the priests maintain the moral and ideological balance and order (magicians may be needed on occasion to alter the existing order).

The military, or second, function has the responsibility of protecting the society from those forces which would be outside aggressors or those which could be internal disrupters of the divinely ordained order.

Producers ensure that there is plenty of everything— goods and services needed by the society to keep it running in a prosperous way.

Management, security and work—these are three principles that can be derived from the three functions of the Gods and their socioeconomic reflections.

In the Germanic pantheon the first function finds Tyr in the capacity of king and Odin in that of the priest/magician. In most Indo-European societies kingship is the supreme aspect of the first function, but in the Germanic society the priest magician is given supremacy. Tyr rules over the goal of seeking right (or justice) in our lives— of being logical in our judgments, while Odin rules over the goal of wisdom (or intelligence) in our experience. Odin is the supreme God in the Germanic pantheon, because he is best able to combine all other elements and goals of the conscious beings of the Universe.

Thor is the God of the second function— the soldier who is always out in the east on a never-ending campaign against the enemies of the order of consciousness and nature established in Midgard and Asgard. He rules over the goal of seeking *might* or inner strength in our lives.

Frey and Freya, the Lord and Lady of the Vanir, most typify the third function as the God and Goddess of plenty, fertility and prosperity. These Vanic deities rule over the three goals of seeking harvest, frith and love— or prosperity, peace and pleasure in our lives.

As you read the myths of the Gods and Goddesses, you will begin to find that some myths and some Gods have a special attraction for you. These are the myths and Gods you should give attention to first and are the ones most likely to be of use to you. For most of us, there are some myths that are always sources of strength and guidance. Because of the Odian bias of the Eddic sources, many of the myths that seem perfect otherwise might be given an interpretation, or make a point that does not ring true to your own soul. Remember that the same myth may tell several stories— to teach many different lessons. The stories are all true. It is up to us to find the interpretations that ring true to our own souls. When you find contradictory versions of compelling myths, choose the one that rings true to you. There is no one "real" and "right" version of any of the myths.

In ancient times variations occurred naturally as a result of tribal and functional attitudes. Certain deities were worshipped in some regions and not known in others in the elder days. It is the task of the Elders to try to determine which meanings were intended by the teller of a myth in ancient times and which interpretations are most likely to have been accepted and by whom. Though traditional interpretations may serve as guides, it is now our work to find the meanings that make the Gods and the faith most real in our lives today. If a tradition is alive it is natural that it will grow and change.

The kinds of Gods one chooses as patrons has much to do with the kinds of activities by which an individual derives a sense of identity. To many people this will be linked to their lines of employment and/or family. If someone has a sense of having a life's work, patron deities relating to this work will likely serve as sponsors. Others may find an affinity for a particular God or class of wight on the basis of an attraction to the essential character of the God or wight. Here let us think about the ways in which certain lines of work may be linked to certain Gods and wights.

The Vanir

Frey and Freya are nearly as universally loved as Thor. Frey and Freya are members of a class of Gods known as the Vanir (or Wanes). The Vanir are the Gods concerned primarily with harvest (prosperity), frith (secure peace), and love (pleasure). They are the Gods of production and of the enjoyment of the produce. They are the generators of material goods and eagerly acquire money, material gain, and pursue the pleasures of the flesh.

Frey seems somewhat more concerned with harvest and frith, while Freya is especially concerned with love. Freya is also concerned with a wide variety of other things, including magic and warfare.

Freya

Freya, like Odin, is a seeker of wisdom and a magician. Her penchant for eroticism is well known and in fact linked to her other passions for wisdom and magic. Like her brother, Frey, she is no stranger to wealth. Of all the Goddesses, Freya seems to have the greatest following in the current phase of the revival. Her attraction seems to be greater perhaps than that of any other deity in the pantheon. She had quite a following throughout Scandinavia during the Viking Age as well.

Mystics, artists poets, visionaries, diviners and the like are among a few who might find an attraction to Freya.

Frey

Obviously the goals of this class of Gods is most in synch with those of the vast majority of people in our society today. This is as it always was. The winning of wealth and the pursuit of pleasure, if conducted in the context of the six-fold goal and the nine noble virtues, are good and holy things in and of themselves. The work of the Vanic type of people should bring prosperity and pleasure to all. In seeking wealth we can create it. It is the sacred function of the Vanir to see to the prosperity of the whole society. There are a number of different types of Vanic deities as there is a wide variety of paths to these same goals. The banker and the farmer alike may both find a friend in Frey, though the farmer may find Nerthus or Erce, the Earth-Mother, to be a closer friend. While bankers may find Niord to their liking as his interests are more clearly bound up with commerce and trade— especially international trade. Working folk, crafts and trades people of all sorts may find a friend in Frey if their trade or company is not already under the ægis of another patron.

People involved in the automobile industry or equestrian activities will likely relate well to Frey. Frey is a God of wagons as well as horses, so heavy farm equipment or trucking and transportation or freight and even road building equipment might come under his ægis.

Niord

Frey's father, Niord, is a God of maritime activity especially when this is of a commercial kind. Although he is also a God of fishermen and other naval activity. Any merchant, especially ones involved directly or indirectly with overseas merchandise may find Niord a friendly patron.

The Æsir

Thor has been the most popular God in the 20th century reemergence of the Troth. This may have much to do with the popularity of Thor in Iceland in the Viking Age and his consequent prominence in the Eddic material. Thor is the Soldier of Asgard. But in Iceland he was popular with everybody and has come to be known to us through the Icelandic sources as an honest, simple, hard-working hard-fighting, hard-drinking yeoman/soldier. Thor is the God of Might. Might is the power that sustains and expands the current world order. It provides the capability for victory and defence. The work of Thor is to protect Gods and men alike. Thor's work requires giving great trust and loyalty in causes affecting the whole society. Thor risks life and limb to protect all the society of the Gods and men— not just his own immediate family. This is much like the soldier who risks his neck for his whole country. Thor is known for his trustworthiness and honesty. He is truthful and loyal to friends but merciless with enemies. He is unflinching and steadfast in all his work.

Of the nine noble virtues, Thor is the exemplary model for heartiness, truth, troth and steadfastness. Thor takes his greatest pleasure in his great works. Though he can likely out-drink any two of the other Gods together, he is basically a very sober sort who wields his might only in anger. When the other Gods are gathered to share in feast and sumble, Thor is typically in the East slaying Etins until there is trouble. Though he protects the frith and frolic of the others, he is not happiest in the enjoyment of these things. Thor's great feats of eating and drinking likely take place more often in the field or in the camp than in the halls of Asgard. He is also very much a family man. He has never been accused of breaking troth with his wife, Sif, or with anyone else for that matter.

Thor is generally popular and revered for his strength and his unwavering steadfastness in his duty and living of the nine noble virtues. Thor is a natural choice for career military personnel and veterans.

Tyr

Tiw or Tyr is the God of the maintenance of social order. He is about effective organization for the purpose of facilitating the smooth running of society's administrative machinery. Tyr is the God of law and of the law-thing or court of law.

Tyr represents sacrifice on behalf of society and the maintenance of order and the status quo. Tyr gave his right hand to restrain the forces that lead to change in the form of an eventual Ragnarök. Folk involved in legislation, administration of justice, law enforcement, management and science will likely be able to relate to Tyr. Judges, politicians, lawyers, people in law enforcement, and those involved in work that requires careful and critical thinking such as scientists and certain other types of academicians are often followers of Tyr. If money is your greatest pleasure resulting from your work, you may find Frey or Niord more to your liking.

Frigga

Frigga is a Goddess involved in domestic activities such as child rearing and running a household will do well to think on the doings of Frigga. Though she is not often in the forefront in the myths, she has a powerful behind the scenes influence. In her relationship with Odin she sometimes seems to be the wheel behind the wheel who is really responsible for the outcome of events in which her legal husband is involved in the webs of intrigue she spins. She is subtle, yet influential. Those involved in family counseling, social work, and elementary education may find a friend in Frigga. Those in work relating to the fabrication and repair of clothing may also look to Frigga for a sponsor (she is known in the mythology as a spinner and weaver). Other arts generally considered to be of domestic origin, such as cooking, may also be devoted to her.

Heimdall

Heimdall is the watchman of the Gods. He usually sits in a hall at the head of the cosmic Bifröst Bridge looking out and listening over the worlds— he is especially watchful for the enemies of Asgard and Midgard such as Etins and the armies of thurses which herald a great Ragnarök. Though he is generally involved in surveillance and security work, Heimdall is also known to take an active role in conducting investigations— he retrieved the Brisingamen (Freya's magical necklace) from the clutches of Loki and fought with him in the shape of a seal. Tyr is the God of mainly high level administration, Heimdall is more concerned with field work and actually implementing the laws legislated by Tyric folk. Heimdall's people are more "hands-on." Professions falling under his ægis might include intelligence, private and public investigation, police work, detective work, security work and such. Those working with surveillance equipment, alarm systems and the like may also find their work an echo of that done by Heimdall.

Odin

Odin is the God of creative inspiration and the spirit of inquiry and the divine madness that has driven our folk to make great strides in theoretical science and technology, art, poetry and in so many other things. Odin more than any other God is a seeker of wisdom, and as such he has more of it than any one else. His advice (rede) is therefore greatly valued. In leadership he functions as an advisor, in battle as a strategist or general. It is the Tyrists and Thorists who implement the designs of the Odian. Odin synthesizes the information gathered by the God Heimdall and abstracts it into plans and briefs for the Tyrists and Thorists, and for all the other Gods and Goddesses in their special functions. The role of the Odian in society is that of the theoretical thinker (philosopher) and artist.

Many of the same professions covered by Tyr will be covered by Odin— the main difference is in the *personality* of the individual. The Odian will usually be one who is more *creative* and who breaks new territory, while the Tyrist is one who maintains the way things are and keeps them running right. This difference, of course, leads to many conflicts— most of which have a constructive result if they are understood in this divine context.

Eira

She is the Goddess sponsoring those who are involved with the healing arts— doctors, herbalists, dieticians, and so on.

Saga

This Goddess is the sponsor of historians, bards, storytellers and so on.

Forseti

A God who puts lawsuits to sleep. Some lawyers and litigators may be well disposed toward Forseti— or perhaps not.

Syn

She is also to be called in the event of lawsuits. This Goddess looks to prevent an unjust judgment from being brought out.

Dwarves or Dark Elves

Though the Æsir fashioned forges and tools in the earliest of times, there is no known wight among the Æsir and Vanir so skilled in craftsmanship as the dwarves. These entities are usually said to dwell in the earth and in rocks and caves. They are also known as the Dark Elves. Practically all the great tools, weapons or other fabrications owned by the Gods were fashioned by these dwarves. Thor's hammer, the magical ship Skithbladnir and the Brising necklace were all made by Dark Elves. Weyland the Smith was of dwarf kin, as was Regin who reforged Sigurd's sword Gram.

There are many other Gods and wights in the Germanic pantheon who may also function as patron deities or as family or clanic Gods. As you meditate on the Gods and Goddesses of the Troth you will find the meaning and functions of the various divinities and see how they relate to your own life.

Chapter 4
WIGHTS OF THE HOUSE AND GARDEN

A survey conducted about the time that President Ronald Reagan visited Reykjavík showed that about half of the people living in Iceland have seen elves and such wights and that about three quarters of the population believes in them. Heathens who go to the ancient Teutonic motherlands often report a profound sense of connectedness with the living soil and the presence of the spirits of the land, of the landwights, the elves and the dwarves. These "spirits" are closely associated with natural areas, particularly ancient holy sites, fields and gardens, and more importantly for us the household and hearth itself. The spirits of the land and household remain one of the great bastions of resistance and will not die until the very folk itself and its soul are destroyed.

Though their presence is not as strong in the New World, they are here, but it takes especially sensitive people to notice. As surely as the Gods and wights are part of our own souls, they have followed us across the Atlantic and dwell in our own households and hearths. This can be said to have happened because the wights actually emanate from the soul or psyche of the folk to which they are attached. When the Norwegians came to Iceland in the late 9th century the wights came not so much "with them" as "from within them."

The hearth and the stove tend to harbor the most useful household wights. Typically the hearth, which also served as the cooking area in ancient times, as the focus of the household cult and worship. From folklore and personal experience, I have found that things fare best in a household if at least nominal attention is given the wights. If ignored or offended they may cause a good deal of mischief, but if they are honored they can help things to run smoothly and even to bring great luck and prosperity. For those who are aware of, capable of perceiving them, even greater gifts may be had.

In most households they tend to be ignored and if they are perceived at all, they are typically interpreted as evil spirits and a source of terror. This ignorance is largely the result of the propaganda of the Church. Though they are generally beneficent and of great use in the household and yard, they can be mischievous and even downright dangerous when they are ill-disposed. Their mischief has traditionally been thought to cause household accidents, illnesses, destruction of property and even death. Treating them as though they were evil is likely the greatest source of their ill-will. But if you are going to encourage their presence, you need to treat them with respect. It is also possible to wind up with wights that are malicious. In this case you should perform the protective working discussed in the chapter on land-taking. You should also ensure that your household is warded against unwanted wights. You do not want a surfeit of spirits any more than you want all the kids and animals in the neighborhood at your home. They are also prone to thievery when ill-disposed. If you find you are missing your keys or some other important possession, try leaving milk and cookies or other goodies or tokens of esteem on the hearth or household stall or shrine. You might set aside a special place on your harrow or hearth for gifts to the wights. These may be left permanently on the harrow or buried in a special place, or handled in some other manner that the wights seem to approve of.

Tompts

In Sweden the hearth and household wights are known as tompts and they are known to enter the household through the hearth, some traditions have them coming in through underground tunnels beneath the hearth. Actual heathen folk, however, do not believe such tunnels to be physically under the earth of the hearth, but see as the hearth stone as a gateway to the spiritual plane of the dwarves or tompts. Other wights, such as elves, are known to enter the household by means of the flames of the hearth or harrow. Elves are known in Scotland and some areas of Scandinavia to enter the household through knotholes in wood and sometimes borne aloft on a sunbeam. The wood of the hearth, the lintel or threshold and other major household furnishings also serve as gateways and homes for elves, tompts and other wights. If wights are known to abide in a threshold, it is advisable not to slam the door unless you mean to wake them or scare them away. Stones have long been known as gateways between Midgard and Dwarf-Home. The stones of the hearth, or the stones upon which the harrow stands are also ancient abodes for household wights. Folklore has long had it that "evil," that is "heathen," spirits dwell beneath the altar stones of churches. A vast number of European churches were intentionally built over ancient heathen holy places in order to prevent people from gathering at these sites for heathen celebrations. A great deal of ancient power lays under the altars of churches and cathedrals everywhere, just waiting for true folk to take out the altars and bring in the holy harrows. Regional folk-traditions may give much information about the nature of the old spirits though bear in mind that these spirits have often been diabolized over the centuries by successful Church propaganda.

By the time most of the tales of the tompts and other household spirits came to be written down, the stove had come to replace the fireplace as the main abode or gateway of the tompts. Even into the 19th century, and likely to this very day, in Scandinavia, it is not uncommon for folks to make offerings of food and beer to the tompts, trolls and elves. Houses that harbor tompts are usually prosperous, clean and orderly. The people in such households are decent with each other and with the tompts. Tompts are happiest if they have a role to play and are paid for it. In many Scandinavian stories the tompts take the shape of ordinary human beings and hire on as servants and expect in payment a bowl of porridge with butter in it. A happy tompt is industrious in contributing to the good mood and well being of the household, though they can get unruly if duly offended and not given proper payment or respect. If you make an agreement with your tompts or promise them payment and allot them duties in a ritual setting, be sure and keep your end of the deal, as long as the tompts keep theirs. If they don't maybe you don't have tompts at all and what you need is to kick the old rascals out and try to invite in a new crew.

The offerings of porridge and butter were typically left on the stove of the hearth. Other offerings have included cheese, bread, and other common household staples. Whatever foods you normally eat should be given to the tompts in daily offerings. If you do not eat porridge, it is probably as well you do not make your tompts eat it. Sometimes special offerings are made on Yule morning made up of such things as tobacco, cloth and a shovel full of earth. If you make daily offerings to the tompts you may simply hallow the gift with the hammer or other appropriate sign and set it on the harrow or stove or dispose of it in the earth.

Elves

Elves are another common wight of the household, as well as of the gardens and fields. There are subterranean elves— and elves of the air. Elves and tompts are often very involved with the affairs of not just a household, but also of the family. This involvement may last over many generations. The elves are often numbered among the ancestors or are known to have made significant contributions to the fortunes of the family at some point. In Scandinavian folklore elves and other wights are said to take on human form and in this fashion to have begotten children on or by humans. This motif is also found in the sagas and Eddas. In the Sagas of Ancient Times, the mythical Icelandic sagas about events in the mythic past, we find purely elven beings having intercourse with human beings and begetting children on them. It is by such intercourse that the seith-woman (magician) Huld was begotten in *Hrolf-Kraki's Saga*. In the Family Sagas, about people and events in historical times, we find people who are known to have had elven or etinish descent but we rarely find stories of interaction between humans and elven folk. In the *Heimskringla* there is a story of a man who refused to convert to Christianity under the pressure of Olaf Tryggvason. He protested that because he was of elven heritage, and thus belonged to a heathen class of *beings,* he could not "convert." He was then summarily tortured to death. Such knowledge has been handed down among some families to this day.

A number of Scandinavian families have elven heirlooms. Among these are drinking vessels, such as cups, bowls and drinking horns. The stories of the acquisition of these items are generally quite similar. An ancestor encounters the elven folk on the road and spends some time with them— sometimes dancing in their subterranean halls. At some point the ancestor will be given a drink in a horn. But as he distrusts the drink he will throw the liquid over one shoulder— where it singes the hair off his horse. He then rushes home absconding with the drinking vessel. In other traditions the vessels are given as gifts. In some stories the wrath of the trolls over the theft results in the ruin of the family. On the other hand many rich households are said to be blessed by the elves.

The refusal to drink is a motif no doubt a distortion introduced by Church propagandists who taught that all such wights were evil and dealings with them would bring only evil. One of the most evil acts of all, in the eyes of the Church, was the sharing of food and drink with such wights. This is the act whereby the wights and humans exchange and share might and main and bind themselves to each other. This kind of interaction with the elves is especially dangerous from the standpoint of the Church because it makes the drinker forget about the ordinary world and enjoy communion with the elves. This could reach a point where one would not wish to come back from the world of these transmundane wights. Certainly some one who had shared such drink with the elves and gained something from it would not be likely to return to church.

Elves, along with trolls and certain other wights, are associated with changelings— that is, the theft of babies by non-human beings. These wights are reputed to snatch babies out of their cribs and replace them with their own inferior children. This belief seems to be another distortion of another mainstay of the ancient religion and seems to be designed to prevent folks from looking at their native beliefs regarding the acquisition and transference of souls. It seems that the root of the changeling belief is the knowledge that ancestral souls, including those of divine races, may enter a child at or before the time of the naming. In this folkish belief people have been taught to fear elves when it comes to their children. This fear, if it was not instituted by the Church, it was most certainly encouraged by the new religion. Oddly enough, however, in some European folk-traditions clergymen have been said to be goblins and children are warned to watch out lest the parson boil them in a pitch pot.

Beliefs in things such as changelings is the most likely origin for the idea that elves could take on human shape. It is simply that the human form (body) acquired a elven soul (haming or fetch) at or near the time of birth. But it is also possible that such an acquisition could take place at later stages in life. This is what is happening in the folk tales regarding adults who visit the hidden land of the elves and are offered a horn of mead. These visits usually take place during trance-journeys or dreams or other mystical or magical experiences. It is in this way that tompts, trolls, etins and others may be numbered among your ancestors.

In more rationalistic terms the beliefs surrounding changelings may also be seen as mythic interpretations or models meant to explain such phenomena as mental retardation or other genetic defects simply inherited in an unpredictable way from the ancestors — from the elves, if you will.

In the Middle Ages small bows, arrows, shoes and things a child might play with were often left in a special place in the cellar of the house for the elves. This was done to encourage them to do good turns for the household.

Elves love music and dancing. Circular patches of grass that are greener than other grass are known as elf rings and are thought to be the places where the elves dance at night. If you want to encourage the presence of elves you might set up rings of stones or fertilize the grass in a ring shape near your outdoor harrow. This will create an environment hospitable to them.

They are also known to like harp music and fiddles. The dances they perform are not likely to differ too much from the round dances of the European folk traditions. Incidentally, this type of dance was banned by the Church for years due to their heathen origin. These dances are typically performed in a circle moving widdershins (counter clockwise) with partners spinning in a deosil (clockwise) direction. Scandinavian folk dances are excellent models. But so too is the central European waltz.

Other Wights

Into the modern era elf harrows were set up in Sweden for magical workings to heal the sick. Women known as harrow-wives tended these altars. In workings for the sick they would divine whether the sickness had been inflicted by the elves, and if so what kind of infliction it was. This kind of illness is commonly known as "elf-shot." This is because it is believed that the elves can shoot invisible magical projectiles into the soul of a person and cause illness. The harrow-wives would smear the stones of the harrow with swine fat and would sing prayers over the stones. On the harrow itself they would have three metal shavings of some ancestral object belonging to the afflicted. They would then pour boiling lead into a bowl of water and scry the source of the illness. If it is determined that elves indeed caused the illness, then they would do a healing working at the harrow on the following Thursday at sunset. These workings are called "striking downs" or "anointings for the elves."

These "harrow-women" (they have been known by other names as well) are likely the modern descendants of the spæ-wives of the Viking Age. The use of swine fat suggests an association with the Goddess Freya. Seith was a magical form that much involved the calling of land-wights and they were frequently called through the singing of prayers or other incantations.

Trolls are another common wight of the European folk. These have been especially diabolized by Church propaganda, but can be as beneficent as elves and tompts if given proper respect. Their main kind of mischief seems to be the stealing of beer and ale. This is the sort of gift that makes them most happy. Just don't give them ale in a vessel with a Christian cross on it— this will not make them happy at all. Trolls are not as house-oriented as tompts, or as elves can be. They are more apt to be found in the fields or under bridges in the country or in town. In Scandinavian lore they are especially linked to mounds and small hills which serve as their gates between Midgard and Etin-Home. Such mounds are also often associated with elves. In the heathen age burial mounds were typically seen as gateways into the underworldly homes.

Dwarves, or Dark Elves, are another kind of wight to survive in folklore and to be honored in folk tradition. They are especially associated with mountainous regions and dwell in the hills. The dwarves are also known in Old Norse as *svart-* or *dökk-álfar* ("black-" or "dark-elves"). They are said to dwell down below Midgard in Svartalfheim. Their main function is that of craftsmen or fabricators of physical reality. They are the ones who shape the forms that find their way to Midgard. They are always thought to be the makers of all sorts of magical objects— they made the Freya's Brisinga-men, and Frey's ship Skithbladnir, for example. In the everyday household cult they can be considered the reabsorbed ancestral skills and crafts expressed in a mythic form. Dwarves are the spirits of craftsmanship— although in later popular terminology the word "elf" was used for both elves and dwarves.

Dises (ON *dísir*, sg. *dís*) are a class of female land-wights that were highly honored in the Viking Age. They are feminine counterparts to elves. If we go back to the most ancient time, there would be no female "elves"— just dises. Of all of these entities, the dises perhaps enjoyed the most active level of cultic attention. Two of the main public holy festivals in the Troth, Winter-Nights and Disting, are especially dedicated to them— and secondarily to the elves.

Dises ensure the on-going wealth and fertility of the household. They keep the children safe and the household healthy and in good working order. Dises are not known by individual names, rather they are always referred to as a collective body. In a way they form a part of a parallel social universe— along with the elves and related entities.

In some ways the dises can be seen as beings quite similar to the *bansidhe* [banshee] in the Irish and Scots tradition.

The land-wights are spirits that spæ-women, volvas, and seith-folk will want to become most familiar with. These are the spirits they work with in divinatory and magical work. Those who intend to work with seith should have some facility for dealings with land wights. Just being able to sense and be aware of the presence of the wights is relatively unusual in the modern world. For many the ability is simply latent, or forgotten. There seems to be some variety in the kinds of subjective experiences people have with wights, but folks who know them generally have a knack for just feeling their presence and personalities. Those who spend much time in communion with wights may be able to gain knowledge they can verbalize and may learn to scry into hidden matters— or, as so often in this day and age, just flat go mad or at least become rather "flaky." It may be a hard road back to lost knowledge and many seekers may wind up way off balance, but everyone deep into sorcery is aware that he or she is risking sanity.

The land-wights are the class of wights closest to the hearth after the ancestral spirits. Indeed, they may be ancestral spirits. As a result of the assault on the tradition mounted by the Church much of the lore has been grossly twisted and distorted. Nevertheless, enough remains that through work we may bring the friendly wights of the land back to our hearths and harrows.

Chapter 5
HOUNDS, HINDS AND FELINES

The animals you choose to live with can affect your life as much as the company you choose to keep and the people you choose to live with. They too contribute to the collective soul of the hearth as do the people who live there, the furnishings and the art. Pets are part of the family. Here we shall consider the lore of animals and their role in the true household.

Each kind of pet has it own "energy" or "influence." This influence blends with the energies of everything else in the household to create the overall mood of the household. In choosing components of the household you can harmonize various elements to create powerful and effective spiritual chords that resonate positively in the hearts and minds of all who experience the household— that is when the choices are made in a conscious or holy manner. If properly coordinated the entities in your house will find themselves in the right mood in the right time and the energies will be right to dynamize their souls to do the right thing at the right time.

When integrating pets into your household you might consider their associations with the holy Germanic folklore and mythology.

The kinds of animals most closely linked with the household, the dog and cat are both associated with Freya, as are certain farm animals. Though the dog is linked with Odin as a relative of the wolf and can be connected with other deities for its function in the hunt. That animals characteristic of the household should be associated with Freya (and perhaps also Frigga) is logical seeing that in the Viking Age the household was the domain of women and the wife was the chief manager of the house.

The cat's association with Freya is well established by Eddic sources and the role of cats as the escorts and familiars witches (Freya's Folk) is known throughout the Middle Ages.

The most Nordic or Germanic breed of cat is the Norwegian Forest Cat (*Norsk Skogkatt*). It is a large breed mentioned in Scandinavian folk tales and legends for the past several hundred years. The Forest Cat is very similar to the Main Coon Cat more common in this country. The breed has been recognized as an official one among cat fanciers in Norway since the 1930s, although the first breeding pair was not brought to America until 1979. This type of cat is a rugged outdoor animal and can stand extremes of climate. It is a bold hunter but also loves human company— and will even take walks along side its master like a dog. The Forest Cat is not a domesticated wild cat, but is the result of unplanned breeding in a harsh environment.

Most of the sacrificial animals were domestic herd animals or wild beasts of the hunt. Many are known to be linked to particular divinities, while the associations and significances of others are yet to be revealed.

Naturally it is not practical to keep many of these beasts at our dwellings— at least not for city folk. The animals may be honored and their influence brought into the house with pictures, statues and other objects connected with the beast. This is much like when you bring the power of the Goddesses and Gods into the household through their images. In fact, of course, the animal images are actually potent symbols of the divine forces associated with them. Our ancestors never "worshiped" animals in and of themselves.

Keep in mind the purpose of a given room when you integrate these images into your home. The presence of the owl, for example, might be brought to bear on a study or any room used for nocturnal work or the acquisition of knowledge or wisdom.

Besides association with deities, an animal may have connections with a certain cosmic or psychological realm. Snakes, fish, dragons (wyrms), sharks, and so on, are to be found in the chthonic or underworldly realm of Nifel-Home, Hel and the waters beyond Midgard. These are creatures of the underground, underwater, unseen realms of psychological experience. They may correspond to elements in the unconscious. The greater wyrms, such as Iormungand and Nithhögg, may correspond to aspects of the whole collective unconscious. These are the creatures of the dark side.

Horses, goats, dogs and other four footed mammals are creatures of Midgard. They are beasts of our own realm of existence and being.

Most birds correspond to the heavenly realms of Asgard, Light-Elf-Home and Wane-Home. These are linked to higher conscious states— levels of great and godlike wakefulness and knowledge.

Another thing to think about when considering what animal powers to bring into your home is any known personal, family, or tribal connections of a particular beast. These may be known from family lore, family crests, intuition, and in rare cases from visions obtained through inner work or acquired immediately before death. If you are like most people, you are probably not prone to go out of your way to acquire a profound inner vision. You may use intuition and clues given to you in dreams. You might think about traits that characterize certain animals and the sorts of people who manifest these traits and on what kinds of characteristics are strong in your own personality.

The importance of horses in ancient society cannot be overemphasized. They were the equivalent of the automobile. They provided transportation and prestige. In the mead hall athelings talked endlessly of their horses. In ancient Germanic society the horse was perhaps the greatest and holiest of sacrificial beasts. In the sagas you can read of sacrificial horse meat served at the *blótar* (blessings) of in the halls of kings. In early Indo-European culture the horse was used as a symbol or substitution for a human being in sacrifices. Our modern abhorrence for horse meat is a result of strict penalties on the consumption of horse flesh by the medieval Church in an effort to destroy one of the mainstays of public heathen sacrifice. Tradition has it that England was founded by Hengest and Horsa ("Stallion" and "Horse").

The horse is especially important in the cults of Frey and Odin. The best of horses in Norse mythology is Odin's eight-legged steed, Sleipnir. The other Gods also have special horses. *Freygoðar* ("priests of Frey") used to keep unridden and unbroken horses hallowed to their God. From the first century sacred horses are known to have been kept for purposes of divination, as well as for eventual sacrifice. The priests and priestesses who looked after these horses would take omens from their whinnying and frothing and other behaviors.

After horses, cattle were most widely revered. If the horse was the automobile, cattle were at least tractors. Cattle had served as units of monetary wealth (mobile property) in the most ancient of times. Our word "fee" is derived from the Proto-Germanic word for cattle: *fehu*. This is the name of the first rune. In later times, when precious metals took over the function of mobile wealth, money was called "fee." Cattle, obviously connected with Frey by their association with wealth are very much a part of the cult of the Vanir— especially Frey. Drinking horns and leather products may all serve as symbols of this animal.

The boar may be connected primarily with Freya. But also with Frey and Odin. Both Frey and Freya ride boars— one fashioned of gold by the dwarves. The wild boar or yesteryear was not the domestic pig of today. Wild boars were known as the most dangerous beasts in the forest. The boar Sæhrimnir is devoured by the Einherjar in Valhalla each night and made whole again in the morning.

For those who would like the experience of relating to a porcine creature — for by relating to a creature sacred to a divinity you can understand that divinity on a much deeper level than would otherwise be the case — you might consider getting a pet pig. The small so-clled Vietnamese potbellied pig would be an ideal choice, as the large domesitc breeds would be overwhealming. Even the potbellies, which may be only fifty pounds, can be quite a challenge to the unaware owner. They are only motivated by food. They do not act to please their "masters." They are creatures of habit. If you do not get your pig in the habit of doing what you want it to do— it will run over you land do as it pleases.

The goat is most especially linked to Thor, though it seems also to have had links to the Vanir as well. The goats that drew Thor's chariot could be sacrificed and eaten and hallowed with his hammer and made whole again in the morning.

The concept of an animal being sacrificed, eaten, and restored to wholeness again reflects the ancient attitude toward sacrificial animals. They provided sustenance — both spiritual and physical — to Gods and men. Their existence (as a species) was strengthened and constantly renewed by the sacrificial act— so the process as a whole was cooperative and restorative. This attitude is typical of the Germanic people as a whole. In ancient times the emphasis was on the survival and health of the *whole* rather than the individual, so the sacrificial act was indeed one which restored the animal (as a whole).

Harts or deer are linked to the dwarves in the lore. It is in the shape of harts that dwarves fare out into Midgard and even into Asgard where they eat from the limbs of Yggdrasill. There are four harts named Dáin, Dvalin, Duneyr, and Durathror which gnaw at the limbs of the World-Tree at the four corners of heaven.

The eagle is one of Odin's animals, as are the other Germanic beasts of battle and carrion— the raven and the wolf. These creatures flock to the scene of battle often before it ever occurs to scavenge the corpses of the slain. By devouring the dead they are redistributing the flesh and spirit in nature and the Nine-Worlds. Those eaten by eagles and ravens might wind up in Valhalla, while those taken by wolves might be reborn in Midgard more readily. The eagle is also a creature of Etin-Home and at least three etins are known to have taken the shape or *hamr* of an eagle when faring forth.

The raven is one of Odin's animals. While the eagle is noble and strong, the raven is wise, cunning and sorcerous.

The owl may be associated with magic and things hidden. Along with the cookoo, magpie and raven, is linked to sorcery. It is best to speak respectfully of these birds and not to kill them needlessly. Such birds are credited with powerful avenging spirits that cause crippling and fatal accidents.

The cookoo bird is very prominent in Germanic folk traditions concerning magic— and is seen as a sign of the coming of spiring and the renewal of nature.

Fish may be linked to Ran or Niord. Like the snake they are linked with acts of delving into depths of the unknown, bringing the spark of conscious light to shadows of the halls of Hel (Death). Dwarves have been known to take the shape of salmon, as has Loki. Fish — and especially salmon — may be eaten to gain underworld wisdom.

Snakes are beasts of the chthonic realms. Their presence in are and literature as poisonous adders and vipers or as dragons is ever-present. In early medieval Church records there are references to the worship of sacred vipers or snakes among the Danes and the Langobards. The snake motif is found mainly in Nifel-Home and Etin-Home. The two greatest serpents are Nithhögg, who snaps to pieces the roots of the World-Tree, and the Midgard-Worm (also known as Iormungand) who encircles the ocean around Midgard. When Odin sought the mead of poetry housed in Suttung's hall, he took the form of a snake to burrow though the mountain that houses the hall. The snake is linked with the uncanny wisdom of dark and hidden places. As such it has been both feared and revered in the North. Some Scandinavian folklore has it that eating certain kinds of snakes, such as a snake with a crown on its head, gives one the power to see into hidden things.

Bears are creatures of enormous physical power. Some workers of seith-magic are said to have fared forth into combat in bear-shape and to have transformed others into bears. The bear's might is sought by the "bear-shirters" (berserks) of Odin who would wear bear-skins into battle and fall into supernatural battle rage that endowed them with such strength and fury that they were actually shape-shifted into bears. The bear is found in many common Norse names such as Bera and Björn.

Wolves are also Odin's animals. A Swedish tradition has it that when animals spoke, the wolf said: "Call me warg and I will be wroth with thee!" Wild and dangerous predators were often called by euphemisms or circumlocutions rather than by their rightful names in order not to invoke them. The same was done with the bear— all the name really means is "the brown one." People walking through the dark woods thought that if they just used the true name of the animal it would tend to call it to them— which was usually not a desirable thing. Thus the true names became "tabuized" and sometime s lost in time.

Warg is a term for "wolf" that can also mean "outlaw." In Old Norse an outlaw might be known as "a warg among holy places" (*vargr í véum*).

The following is a list of other respectful names for various animals in Swedish tradition:

Fox: Blue Foot, or He that Goes in the Forest
Bear: The Old One or Grandfather
Rat: The Longbodied
Mouse: The Small Grey
Seal: Brother Lars
Wolf: Gold Foot or Grey Foot or Grey Tosse— but not Warg

Some folks are inclined to seek out Teutonic breeds of animals for the household and farm. The Norwegian Elkhound is a pan-Scandinavian breed of dog. The Elkhound is more closely related to the wolf than any other domestic dog. Elkhounds are exceptionally loyal and dependable. In Norway and Sweden they are still used to hunt moose. The Norwegian word *elghund* really means "Moose Dog." It is not really a "hound" in the usual sense. The Great Greys have a long and noble history of service and hunting, rescue, herding and other commendable activities. They make poor police or attack dogs, however. They seem to have affinities with humans that lie too deep.

February 14, 1842 is still remembered in the Norderhove Valley of Norway as one of the Great grey's finest hours. This was a true "Wolf Age" and this night is called "Wolf Night." Norway was at this time being over run by packs of hungry wolves perhaps driven to desperate action due to the severity of the winter. At one farm stead there lived a pack of nine tough Elkhounds. The pack was led by Fanarok, the toughest of them all. One of Fanarok's brothers, Purven, was made a house dog because he was small. In spite of their different life styles— one a mighty hunter the other a loving pet — the two were fierce friends. One night when Fanarok was locked in the barn to guard the cattle, his little brother accidentally got locked out of the house where he normally spent the night. In a short while a roving pack of hungry wolves came upon the farm stead and tore little Purven to shreds within earshot of Fanarok who struggled heroically against the sturdy craftsmanship of the old Norwegian barn makers. When Fanarok finally got free, all he found were bits of fur in the mud and blood stained snow. Fanarok at once led his band of loyal Elkhounds to set up an ambush in the woods. He ran out alone and lured the wolves into the trap where the hounds attacked. The great din of the battle brought out the local farmers armed with axes and swords. At the end of the fray 27 were counted victims of Fanarok's vengeance.

There are several other dog-breeds important to Germanic tradition and lore. Some of these include the Rottweiler, the Great Dane and the German Shepherd.

The Rottweiler is actually a breed of oriental (Iranian) origin which was brought west by the Romans. Roman soldiers took these dogs with them on their expeditions to the north, where a large number of them were bred in an encampment near the present-day town of Rottweil in southwestern Germany. These dogs were used for everything from pulling carts to fighting alongside soldiers in battle. Today they are noted for their aggressiveness, but properly socialized they make wonderful companions. They are gentle with things weaker than themselves, but often aggressive and competitive with other large dogs.

The Great Dane, or *Dogge*, as the Germans call them today, were the breed the Vikings took with them on their raids. They were often used as "shock-troops" against those who might try to defend themselves from the raiders. For anyone who has known a Great Dane, this history is perhaps difficult to believe, as they are among the most gentle of breeds today.

The German Shepherd is perhaps one of the best known of the northern European breeds. They are unmatched for intelligence and for being cooperative with human masters. This is what has made them a favorite of police forces around the world. No dog will work harder, longer, or with more enjoyment for his task than the German Shepherd— even if they think "work" is chasing a ball or stick across the yard.

Folk tradition also provides lore on means of protecting your animals from diseases and accidents or to keep them from running away. Most of this involves preventing elf-shot and bad relations with the local wights as well as enlisting the help of such wights in curing afflictions. There are, of course, numerous folk remedies. One old custom of the health of cattle required running them between two Easter or Midsummer fires. A custom for keeping cats requires the owner to chase the cat around the room three times.

Chapter 6
WELCOME TO THE MACHINES

Animysticism

The inanimate objects of your household have moods and "energies" of their own. They have "personalities," if you will. Art and furniture all make their contributions to the feeling of the household. In so-called primitive or traditional societies inanimate objects are often considered to have a soul, to have personalities of their own. This kind of thinking is known to anthropologists as "animism." Objects may also be thought to contain "energies" but to have no real personality. This kind of thinking is known as "dynamism." Though we know that machines and inanimate objects do not really have thoughts and feelings, they nevertheless have their own idiosyncrasies which we might characterize as "personalities" or "energies." Sometimes it is just more convenient or efficient to think of them in this way when we are interacting with them on a regular basis.

Interacting with machines as if they were living beings with thoughts and feelings can make it easier to understand them and to relate to them effectively. It also makes it easier to understand what kind of effect the machine is having on the mood of the household, to feel what kind of "energy" it is projecting.

Machines are art. They are expressions of a human beings subjective, internal vision. Like any tool, they become extensions of our own personalities, or that of the household. Thereby they acquire personality or mood from us and from our living quarters. By being with us, a machine can acquire its own peculiar traits from the way we do or do not use it, from the way we maintain and repair it, from modifications we might make to it, from the way we allow it to manifest unexpected latent qualities acquired in the design of the room, at the factory or in shipping. Like anything in a household, a machine can transform, and be transformed by, the moods of the people in the household.

Machines can actually work better and more harmoniously when you think of them as living beings. This is partly because we become more aware of them and more attentive to them. If we think of machines as living beings they become more subject to manipulation through "magical" acts or prayer as a result of a profound subjective link that may be formed as a result of such interaction. As with all such "magical" activities, it is best not to take one's self too seriously in doing so. Many people have a tenancy to get carried away and take these beliefs and practices a bit too far.

The idea is to make life more efficient and enjoyable, not to become paranoid or totally "whacked out." If you find yourself being more "worried" about your car or washing machine than you were before, you've gone a bit too far. There is a fine line between magic and superstition. There is even a finer line between magical thinking and forms of schizophrenia. One of the defining characteristics of psychotic thinking is the idea that one's own inner experience has a direct effect on the objective world. At the same time this kind of thought is often engaged in among healthy children— the adult can balance this with objective reality and have the world of the eternal child and the adult within— gleaning the practical benefits of both kinds of thought. Our rede on this matter is: Have fun and watch out!

Part II
Worship

Chapter 7
BLESSINGS

A Book of Troth holds the most thorough treatment of the public celebration of the rituals of the Troth available. Here we will review the structure and meaning of the blessing and sumble and talk about them as household activities rather than public events.

The blessing is a ritual giving of gifts to the Gods and the raising of our consciousness to receive their eternal gifts in return. This is the essence of what our forebears called "sacrifice." It is a ritualized and often symbolic sharing of food, drink along with luck, might and main with the Gods and Goddesses and with our kith and kin both in Midgard and beyond. Briefly the Gods or other wights are called to attend the occasion and food and drink are hallowed and loaded with the might and main of the Gods and men alike. This is then distributed in a holy manner among the folk.

The following formula provides the structure for blessings. You may adapt the blessings used in *A Book of Troth* or you may use the ninefold plan to organize your own style of blessings. The main thing is the over all *structure* of the rite— which is the one handed down through the tradition. Your own blessings may be as elaborate or as simple as you wish and may not included features such as a feast, dancing, or dramas within the blessing or after it. Private household rites tend to be simple and small, while public ones tend to be more elaborate and grand. The purpose and effect of both remain the same.

The Blessing Formula

1. Hallowing: Here the ritual space is made holy and the celebrants enter into a holy frame of mind, into the holy time/space, into a mythic frame of reference where myths and the archetypes they represent are imminent.

2. Reading: A myth is read or retold to connect the blessing with a particular mythic form or event.

3. Rede: Meaning is given to the myth by reading or recitation in which the myth read in the reading is linked to the purpose of the blessing. The reading tends to be in a poetic or evocative form, while the rede is more prosaic and straightforward.

4. Call: This is essentially an invocation to the Gods and Goddesses or other transmundane wights who are invited to share in the blessing.

5. Loading: The food and/or drink is filled with the holy might and main of the Gods and men blended together.

6. Drinking or Eating: The godly might is ingested and circulated within. The drink is poured from a horn in which it was loaded into the vessels held by individual celebrants. One of the participants will usually be responsible for distributing the holy liquid. Before drinking it is customary for each person to make the sign of the hammer or some other holy sign over the horn.

7. Blessing: The remaining portion of the drink is poured from the horn into the blessing bowl. An evergreen sprig is dipped in the drink and used to sprinkle or "bless" the harrow and the gathered true folk.

8. Giving: The bowl is emptied and given to divinity. It is usually emptied on the ground to the east of the harrow.

9. Leaving: The work is declared done and the gathered folk return to their ordinary frame of mind.

The Sumble

The sumble is a drinking ritual that may accompany a blessing or stand on its own. At sumbles a horn is passed around among the gathered folk. The leader of the sumble hallows the horn and makes a toast, boast or oath. After this he passes it to the person to his right. Sometimes the folks are seated according to rank and receive drink in that order. As each receives the horn he or she has the opportunity to speak a toast or make an oath. Toasts are typically made in honor of ancestors or Gods and may be accompanied by stories or myths.

In experience of the original Irminsûl Hof in Austin, Texas, the sumble has produced some profound magical atmospheres. When it works well, the gathered folk find themselves in touch with the divine and their words inspired and wise. The words of one often spark inspired thoughts in others such that word leads to word. The wisdom of inspired thought often leads to new understandings that lead to resolve to new action and this is manifested in oaths and boasts. Thus word leads to work. The great works of ancestors as recalled in the context of a sumble can lead to efforts on the part of the gathered folk to match deeds with or emulate the great foremothers and forefathers. Thus work leads to work. The boasts made in a sumble are often not so much a form of bragging about past deeds as they are statements of intent or reports on the results of past oaths, and so on. In a boast you commit yourself to a certain course of action before the gathered folk whose respect you want to have. An oath ring is sometimes kept on the harrow at sumbles for those who want to make a vow on it. It is also traditional to provide an oath block (a small block of wood) on which the oath maker places his right foot when making a vow.

It is not good to get drunk at a sumble or you may find yourself committed to things that you regret the next day. In the *Saga of the Jomsvikings* warriors were tricked into making oaths after being plied with great quantities of strong drink at a feast.

Sometimes an entire sumble is held for a single ancestor or hero or a small group of them. Such sumbles are sometimes known as memory-drinkings. A memory-drinking may go for a single round or more depending on the mood of the group and the decision of the sumble speaker. I there are special shrines or graves for these individuals available, the memory-drinking may be held at that site. At the conclusion some of the ale should be poured out to the honored God or ancestor.

The sumble can follow a fivefold plan or formula:

1. Seating: The folk gather in a circle around a table, a fire or shrine and order themselves with the sumble leader or speaker at the head and close kin or those highest in rank and the eldest will be closest to the speaker in many cases.

2. Bringing the Horn: The individual allotted the bearing of the horn (often called a valkyrie in modern contexts if it is a woman) brings in the horn and the ale. In small gatherings there is often no one person allotted to bearing the horn and it is simply passed from one person to the next.

3. Beginning: The speaker gives a general introduction to the sumble and declares what its special purpose, if any, is to be. The ale is hallowed by the hammer sign and/or words of power that load the ale with divine might and call to mind the purpose of the sumble.

4. Boasts: The speaker is given the first horn and makes the first boast, as described above. The first found is usually given to the Gods and heroes. Different kindreds have different customs in this. Some give the first toast to Odin, the second to Gods and the third to the ancestors and heroes while rounds after that are based purely upon individual inspirations. Another method is to give one round to the Gods, the second to the ancestors and heroes, and a third is left to individual inspiration. Another way is to give the first toast to Odin, the second to Thor, and the third to Frey and Freya and leave subsequent toasts up to individuals. You may use the opportunity to do personal magical work when the horn comes your way.

5. Leaving: After the rounds are complete and the inspiration has waned, the speaker calls an end to the rounds and declares the purpose of the sumble to have been completed.

The sumble and memory-drinking serve to keep the Gods and ancestors alive in our hearts and minds.

Mead, Meat, and Ale

In days of yore both meat and ale were typically consumed at blessings and sumbles. Animals were sacrificed to be consumed at the ritual feast, not to be thrown away. Some parts would be burned off for the Gods, usually parts other than those which humans tended to like to eat.

Nowadays there are very few of us who practice the ritual slaughter of animals. In the old days people knew *how* to ritually slay an animal without torturing it to death. In ancient times it was the practice to be able to slay a sacrificial animal in such a way that it would feel no terror or pain in its death. If this were to be suffered by the animal, it would be indirectly suffered by the God or Goddess who corresponds to the essence of the animal.

Even the few of us with rural backgrounds are incapable of killing an animal in an appropriate manner. Therefore we usually get meat from the supermarket when we want to have meat in our blessing feast.

Liquids such as mead, ale and beer are the most common sacrifices given in blessings. We usually use the best ales and beers available— imported from Germanic countries where possible.

Mead is the most prized drink in sumbles and blessings, but it is also quite rare. There are few commercial meads, such as Merrydown, so we have to brew our own. In Appendix A you will find instructions for brewing your own mead at home. Some folks do not like alcohol and some are opposed to drinking it even in small quantities as a matter of principle. Apple juice may be happily substituted. You may even try non-alcoholic beers.

Wheel of the Year

The Germanic folk ordered time in terms of cycles. The year is a cycle, the day is a cycle, life is a cycle. This is not to say that one year or life is just like another in all respects. While one year will be structured just like another on a cosmic level, there will be variations on the mundane level that radically distinguish one year from another. The effects of these variations carry over from one year to the next creating the apparent linear series of events we call history. The Germanic peoples knew two basic seasons: summer and winter. The greatest festivals of the year tended to occur at the mid-point of the two seasons: midsummer and midwinter. The Teutonic folk had a number of other seasonal festivals. But it is important to know and to remember that historically the seasonal festivals often varied widely from tribe to tribe and from region to region.

The Ring of Troth has adopted the eight spoked division of the holy year. Figure 7.1 shows the approximate tides (periods) during which these festival occasions fall. In ancient times there were varying systems for determining the exact time at which a sacrificial feast would be celebrated. They might be ordered strictly according to the cycles of the moon, or they might be determined by the observation of certain organic or natural events such as the spying of the first swallow or robin of spring, or the blooming of a certain flower in a sacred meadow. Again, the traditions varied from tribe to tribe and from area to area over the whole of the Germanic territory. It is worth remembering that the very survival of our ancestors was often dependant on the correct observation of *organic* events so that they would know the exact timing of certain actions pertaining to hunting and farming, of fishing and herding. These observations were signs of the changing of cycles essential to the physical and economic survival of the folk. The observation of purely mechanical events in the heavens (such as when the sun enters a sign of the zodiac) are largely irrelevant to the actual cycles of nature on this planet.

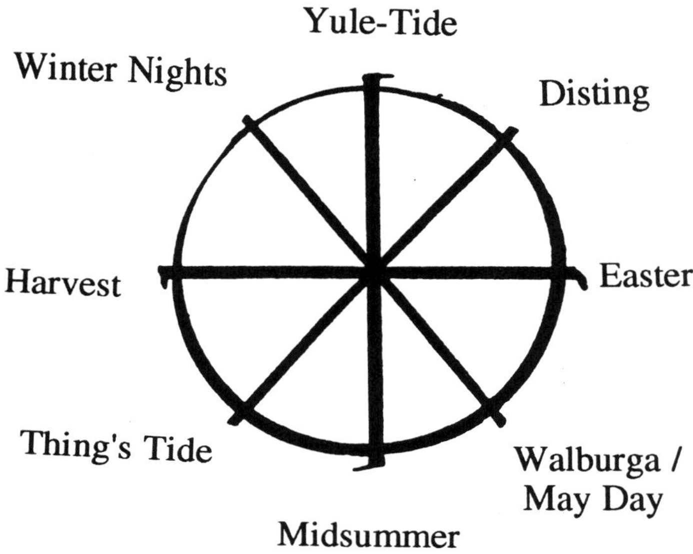

Figure 7.1: Eightfold Timing of the Blessings

Nowadays we usually gather whenever it is most convenient to the most people— usually on a weekend. In this we are simply recognizing the *new fact* of our economic existence: the five-day work week and weekend cycle. The ancient agricultural model of cyclical productivity is certainly more organic, and closer to spiritual truth concerning the cycles of how things "come into being," but the socioeconomic facts of our cultural existences as it *is* today can not be ignored in shaping a practical faith for today and tomorrow which is in harmony with our past.

Full outlines of the performance of these usually publicly held Blessings are given in *A Book of Troth*. Using the ninefold structure supplied on page 138 of that book you can create your own ritual, or, if you have the feel for the performance of Blessings, you can lead a spontaneous form of the more public rituals. In such Blessings the speaker(s) let inspiration guide them and speak as they are moved at appropriate points. When I am working with a small group of familiar people who know how to do Blessings, I often make room at each step of the ritual for the rest of the group to speak as they are moved. Even in the context of written rituals we often allow everyone to contribute to the call by adding calls to Gods left out by other speakers, or by expanding on calls to the Gods and Goddesses already named.

Typically a Hearth will have its own schedule of sumbles and memory-drinkings to heroes and ancestors. Some of the heroes included in the old Ásatrú Free Assembly calendar are: King Radbod of Frisia, Eyvind Kinnrifi, Raud, Ragnar Lodbrok, those who sacked Lindisfarne, Erik the Red, Leif Eriksson and the Einherjar. At the Irminsûl Hof we hold sumbles whose purpose is often not known until we are underway.

The Hammer Working

The Hammer Working is the means by which a stead is hallowed and warded (guarded) for holy work. This sets the stead apart from ordinary affairs to bring on ritual or mythic time and space. At this time participants should enter their highest and most god-like frame of mind.

This is the first part of the blessing and begins with the folk gathered about and the speaker standing at the harrow facing north. The speaker turns clockwise to each of the cardinal directions (east, south, west and back to the north) and makes the sign of the hammer in the air in front of him with a gand (wand), hammer token, or outstretched three fingers. Begin with your arm stretched out slightly above your head pointing north. Draw the gand down to trace the haft of the hammer sign as shown in figure 7.2. See and feel holy power rushing through the gand and into the air. When you have a glowing vertical line before you, draw back your arm and move the gand to the right of the glowing haft and move the gand and trace a horizontal line just under the lower tip of the vertical line to trace the hammer head. Then imagine the completed hammer sign hovering before you. As or after you trace the sign you may repeat a formula such as "Hammer in the north (east, south, west, above, below) hallow and hold this holy stead." There are other formulas used in Odinist circles as well.

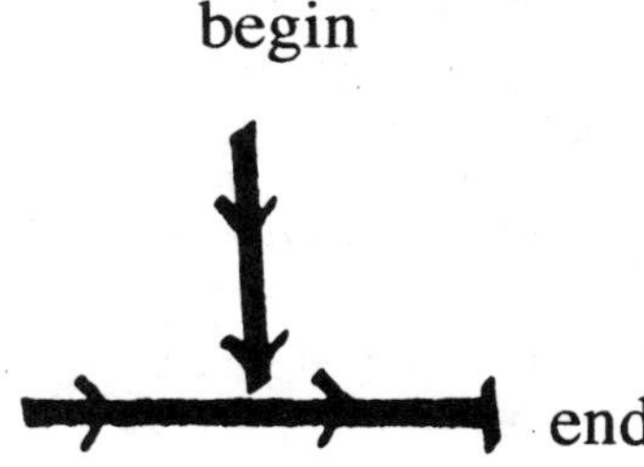

Figure 7.2: Tracing of the Hammer Sign

Signing Sumble

During the blessing and sumbles, it is usual that when the drink comes to you, you sign it with a hammer or another holy sign. This may be done with your fingers, fist, a hammer token, or some other holy sign. The hammer is traced over the drink and hovers over the drink glowing. Feel the might of the hammer flow into the drink. As you drink imagine the might held in the drink filling you up completely with sacred power.

A Blessing for All the Gods and Goddesses

As an example of a complete blessing formula, which can be used for any sacred purpose, such as making a site holy or celebrating one of the Great Blessings (Yule and Midsummer), we present the complete ritual of a formal blessing as used in the Ring of Troth.

1. Hallowing

The hammer-rite is performed, at the conclusion of which the speaker says:

"This stead is hallowed for our work here today (tonight). As the God Heimdall wards the Bifröst Bridge, so this stead is warded against all *unholy wights and ways."

2. Reading (Lay)

A appropriate poem or other reading from the *Poetic Edda* or other mythological source is read.

3. Rede

The speaker says:

"This day (night) we gather together as in days (nights) of yore to greet and honor the Gods and Goddesses who dwell in Asgard. We call upon them to make ripe their might and main in our lives. We call upon them all — the holy many — living as a whole as is Odin's Law."

4. Call

The speaker makes the following calls. After each call, the gathered folk give welcome to the God or Goddesss being called with their name, and add the words: "We give thee welcome!"

Odin, we are awed by they craft,
Tyr, we stay true to thee forever,
Balder, thy brightness and boldness guides us,
Frigga, thy fruit and wisdom keeps us all,
Idunna, thine apples ward our ways,
Thor, thy thunder wards our ways,
Freya, we get freedom from thy frolic,
Frey, from thee we get a harvest of frith.

---

* For a full understanding of the concept of "holy" (and hence "unholy") see Edred Thorsson's essay entitled "The Holy" in *Green Rûna* (pp. 46-50).

Then a litany of divine attributes of the Gods and Goddesses just called is recited by the speaker. After each the gathered folk shot: "We give thee welcome!"

Rune-Lord,
One-handed God,
Holder of the Hringhorn,
Lady of the Gods and Goddesses,
Keeper of the Apples,
Guardian of Asgard,
Holder of the Brisingamen
God of the Wane.

Again we call to you in all your names, be among us here today (tonight) as the have come to give you the gifts of friendship:

Hail all the Gods, hail all the Goddesses,
hail all the holy ones
who dwell together.

5. Loading

The speaker pours mead (or other drink) into the horn, lifts it aloft and says:
"We give you the gifts of our works woven and blended with the might and main of this mead. It lends us — Gods and folk together — help in or striving towards the shining plain where the worlds and wights dwell in wholeness."

6. Drinking

The speaker then drinks from the horn and pours the remainder into the blessing bowl on the harrow or stall. The horn is then refilled and passed to each of the gathered folk. Each makes the sign of the hammer of the rim of the horn before drinking. Each time the remainder of the mead or other drink is poured into the blessing bowl by the speaker.

7. Blessing

The speaker now sprinkles the harrow or stall and the gathered folk with the words:
"The blessings of the Gods and all the Goddesses of our folk be upon us!"

8. Giving

After the blessing is completed, the speaker pours the contents of the blessing bowl out upon the bare ground to the east of the harrow with the words:
"To Odin, Tyr, Balder, Frigga, Idunna, Freya, Frey and to all the Gods and Goddesses of our folk."

9. Leaving

The speaker returns to the harrow or stall and says:
"Thus the work is once again wrought. It renews or hearts to do worthy deeds, and to strive toward our goals with mighty moods, wise words, and trust in our own powers— ever holding our oaths to ourselves and to our folk.!"

Chapter 8
FEASTS, DANCES, DRAMA AND GAMES

In heathen times the major blessings were the tides of the great holidays and celebrations. Blessings were accompanied by great feasts in which the sacrificial foods were eaten. They might also include dances, seasonal dramas, and sacred games. Though many of these events were hardly solemn, they were nevertheless holy. Good cheer and kinship are holy in their own right. Love, frith and good cheer are signs of a successful blessing. Here let us look at ways these pre- and post-blessing festivities are, and can be, made a part of today's Troth celebrations.

The feast typically follows the blessing. These can be as simple or as elaborate as you want. If you do not have the wherewithal to cook an elaborate feast, hallow an ordinary meal. In doing what you *can* you are being *true*. The sacrality will be imparted by its association with the blessing.

If you want to go "whole hog," you can try to coordinate the foods with the theme of the blessing. You might also try to make a feast of traditional European foods. If you want to match your foods with the blessings, consider the season and which holy powers are singled out for special or sole attention during the rite. Look through the Eddas, sagas, and other relevant materials including European folklore to find ideas on food and feasting— especially as it relates to the Gods and season of the blessing.

The major deities are known to have been associated with certain animals, some of them sacrificial animals that were eaten at their blessings. Frey may be connected with any and all foods, but especially those raised in fields where Frey is called upon for good harvest (*ár*). Cattle, boars and horses are animals holy to Frey. Therefore all beef and dairy products, all pork and sausage products, and horseflesh may be featured in feasts dedicated to Frey. Frey is also a God of the fruits of the field. Barley, wheat and other grains may be featured in hallowed breads and cakes.

Freya is elegant and her tastes sophisticated. Pork may be featured in a Freya feast, but you may also find some exotic and expensive foods to honor her. Apples may also be hallowed to honor her. Wedding cakes might be hallowed in her name.

Odin and Tyr may both be honored with horse flesh. In Valhalla the *einherjar* [ayn-her-yar] eat from a great pork at night which regenerates itself during the day. They drink mead and ale. Odin also drinks wine in the fashion southern Europe. Such might be consumed at a feast sacred to Odin.

Thor has two goats which would regenerate themselves after being sacrificed and consumed— that is after they had been properly hallowed by the hammer of the God— Miöllnir [myoll-neer]. These goats once drove his chariot, but they were lamed when a feaster broke open a bone to get the marrow. (The marrow was typically given to the Gods and Goddesses alone. So this is a mythic prohibition against taking what belongs rightly to the

Gods.) Goat meat and dairy products are good for Thor-blessings. Thor is also known to have liked herring and oatmeal.

Frigga is linked to spinning, so it is to sheep and lambs that she is partial.

Idunna would be a great one to honor with apple pie and hot apple cider after the apple harvest. Nuts might also be eaten in her honor as she was brought back from Etin-Home in the form of a nut.

Salmon or other fish might be eaten to honor dwarves or the ancestors.

In honor of Hel (the Goddess of death) you might eat snake.

Other foods of special significance include leeks and related plants such as onions, venison, cranberries and anything taken from your own hallowed garden. Leeks are considered a highly magical plant. Ancient words for leek appear on several runic inscriptions. Cranberries used to be included in ales and meads. Venison is a great meat for sumbles to all the Gods and to honor Sigurd— the greatest hero of our folk who was raised in infancy by hinds. The Gods feast on beasts of the hunt as well as ox, boar, goat, and so on.

To hallow a feast you might simply make the sign of the hammer over it. In fact, each of the feasters might hallow his or her share with the hammer sign. You might also say a short or long prayer over the meal. On the other hand, you might make the entire cooking process into a sacred event and say prayers or loadings over each of the major ingredients and relate them all to the theme of the blessing and even to the other ingredients.

Games

The celebration of major blessings is often accompanied by the playing of games. Numerous games associated with particular holy times have survived in folk custom. Originally they had mythic meaning and religious significance which has been lost over time or been reinterpreted in terms of Christian myths. At one time, sacred games may have been nearly as important to the celebrations as the blessings themselves.

Few of the heathen sacrificial games live on in America other than in isolated communities of Germanic ethnic stock. The Easter egg hunt is one such game practiced nationally in America. Many games have survived into the modern era in Europe. The Troth bases many of its games on these. In the modern revival, kindreds emphasize the physical contests, but contests of wit and wisdom were also much a part of our ancestral celebrations. The typical Ásatrú Free Assembly Althing used to feature an axe throw, a caber toss, and an obstacle course known as the cut and pillage course. For children there was egg toss when the Althing was held at the Easter-tide. The caber toss is a Scottish contest to see who can throw a large heavy pole the farthest.

Most of the games tend to be linked to specific seasonal events and blessings. Such customs as hare pie scrambles, bottle kicking, lifting and hocktide customs and pancake racing or skipping are linked with the Easter event. Bottle kicking is like a number of other street games such as the Haxey Hood game, but it is played with a small iron hooped barrel or bottle.

Two teams of indeterminate numbers, and not necessarily even ones, strive to get a football, bottle — or whatever — to their own goal line. The teams are sometimes made up of rival districts and the goals sometimes two or three miles apart. The game goes on until somebody wins, and this can take several hours.

Wrestling was another common physical contest. In the Viking Age drinking contests were sometimes held at feast. The winner would be expected to hold his drink. Staggering drunk would not do.

According to the Roman historian Tacitus the Germans were so fond of gambling with dice that they would sometimes gamble away their very freedom. For the Germans slavery was generally held to be worse than death, so the wagering of one's freedom was among the greatest of risks. We do not know the exact nature of the early Germanic dice games, but modern ones are in the same spirit.

Lifting is a custom in which women-folk force men-folk into chairs and tie them up allowing them to be ransomed with kisses or money. Hocktide customs involve a day in which women chase down men and tie them with ropes allowing them to ransom themselves with money or kisses. The following day the roles are reversed and men chase women.

In pancake racing women race with a pancake in a pan which they must flip at least three times before reaching the finish line.

Numerous other folk games are practiced throughout Europe and even in some parts of America. These may be recovered from sources such as Gomme's *British Folk-lore*.

Intellectual games include riddle contests, poetry contests, man-matching and lore contests. Riddles were a common means of testing wit among the early Germanic peoples, though the art is little developed today. At some of the Althings there were occasionally folks who would test each other with riddles for hours. The best source for the format for good heathen Viking Age riddles is the *Heidrek's Saga.* It contains the riddles of Gestumblindi. The riddles are presented in the form of a riddle contest between king Heidrek and Gestumblindi, who is really Odin in disguise. These riddles may be concerned with all sorts of natural phenomena, but are all connected with the holy aspects of these things, much like kennings are. A typical riddle from this source goes as follows:

A dweller in the soil
I saw passing
a corpse on a corpse there sat
blind upon blind one
to the billows riding
on a steed without breath it was borne.
This riddle ponder,
o king Heidrek!

Solution: A dead snake on a dead horse on an iceflow floating down a river.

Poetry is currently read more at sumbles than in contests, but as familiarity with the meaning and form of true Germanic poetry increases, so will the occurrence of contests.

The Irminsûl Hof in Austin plays a lore game called Mimir's Head Game that is based on Odin's lore contest with the giant Vafthruthnir (see "Vafthrúthnismál" in the *Poetic Edda*). We typically hold the game in darkness by candle or firelight as we would a sumble. Whoever seems the most versed in lore is designated the chief. The chief has before him a drinking horn that symbolizes his chiefdom. The chief challenges each of the other players with questions or riddles regarding matters of elder lore. Typically we agree to limit the game to a single poem from the *Poetic Edda*. All come prepared. The chief frames a question and asks it of the first person to his right. If that person answers correctly, as judged by the chief, he stays in the circle as a player, if not he has lost his head and participates no more. The chief then asks the second and third and so forth. On the second round, those who answer the chieftain rightly may ask the chief. If the chief answers rightly then he asks the second. If the chief answers wrongly, then he is out of the game and the one who asked the question takes his place. If the chief can go nine rounds without getting knocked out, he is called "the High One." The High One is able to decide which body of lore will be covered on the next session.

The High One is only reduced to the status of chieftain if he is unable to answer a question rightly. The asker of that question may then ask the chief another question to attempt to knock him out and become chief in his stead. If the chief fails he is out, and if he answers rightly he may recover his High One status allowing the challenger to ask him three questions and answering them rightly. He may otherwise recover High One status by going three more rounds as chief. The High One may propose new rules. Each who would challenge the new rules may ask the High One three questions. If the High One answers all rightly, his rule becomes law. We have found that in preparing for these games we wind up knowing the poems quite well. We are proposing that we have a yearly contest in which the game is open to all Eddic lore. We may hold these Mimir's Head Games at national Ostara gatherings.

Dances

The square and round dances of modern European folk dancing are survivals of the sacred dances made around harrows, trees, may-poles and other holy places. Typical of folk dancing is a turning circle of couples who themselves spin clockwise while moving in a large circle that moves widdershins (counter clockwise). Those who know the sacred through ritual work will find that our folk-dances feel like a ritual and give an easy link to the holy frame of mind. No wonder the Church was so adamantly opposed to dancing. By integrating folk-dancing back into our blessings and feasts we will recover and understand the lost language or ritual dance and dramas. If you have the opportunity, experience the polka, and the various forms of German, English, and Scandinavian folk-dancing. Though we can perhaps no longer intellectualize and verbalize the significance of the gestures and motions of the dances, we can feel them, and that is what is most important. In the context of ritual, verbalized meanings are merely another channel to, or link with, the feeling or direct knowledge of the sacred.

Plays

Ancient seasonal and initiatory dramas have survived in folk dramas such as the mumming plays, Morris dancing, sword dancing, and various customs involving the green man, the hobby horse and the Jack in the Green.

The central theme for numerous folk-plays is a combat between two champions and the death and rebirth of one of the champions. Sometimes the combat is over a woman such as the Maid Marion. These are often connected to seasonal festivals celebrating the renewal of the year, but some are also associated with initiatory rites. Dialogs to mumming plays and other folk dramas are recorded in folk lore texts. A number of the dialogs from the poems of the *Poetic Edda* may be adopted to modern holy plays.

Chapter 9
DAILY HOLY WORKINGS

The ways in which we renew our connection with the holy during our daily rounds varies greatly from one individual to another. Some folks have a set of daily workings and/or meditations they do at different times of the day in order to center themselves and renew their awareness of the spiritual in their lives. Others let such awareness come and go as it will. Daily workings encourage a regular realization of the divine and bring increased knowledge of the holy in everyday life.

In *A Book of Troth* daily workings are given for starting a new day, noon-tide, eating and retiring to sleep. Here we wish to expand on the material presented there.

Waking is a good time to get off on the right foot, literally. Putting the right shoe on first, or the left if you prefer, so long as it is done in a conscious and intentional manner, is a traditional way of preparing yourself to be mindful of taking the right steps throughout the day. Put your right foot forward and jump into the fray. As an alternate to the greeting to Sunna given in *A Book of Troth*, you may use the "hailing of Day" given in the "Sigrdrífumál" of the *Poetic Edda*:

Hail Day! Hail the sons of Day!
Hail Night and the daughters of Night!
Look on us with friendly eyes
and give victory to those standing here.
Hail the Æsir, hail the Asynjur!
hail to him on the kind earth!
Grant us healing hands while we live!

As you recite this prayer, strike a posture with your arms lifted on high and spread in a V-shape.

Donning your Thor's Hammer or other holy token should also be done deliberately and perhaps be accompanied by a formula such as "This day shall bring new wonders, great doings, boundless luck and happiness unending— by the might of this hammer!" The activities of the coming day might warrant a special formula to set your being for the work ahead and to call on the strength of the appropriate deities.

The days of the week are dedicated to our Germanic Gods and still bear their names. Tuesday is the day of Tiw (or Tyr), Wednesday is the day of Woden (or Odin), Thursday is the day of Thunor (or Thor), while Friday is the day of Frigge (or Frigga). Monday and Sunday are the days of the moon and sun respectively, while Saturday is named after the Roman God Saturn. In Icelandic Saturday is known as *laugardagur*, which means "washing day." It was customary to bathe and clean things on that day. In principle Saturday can be a day dedicated to a Goddess or another wight of your choosing. The original Germanic week had only five days, so other names were added in more modern times.

You can include an acknowledgment of the deity of the day in your morning formula. During the day you might also look to see the influences of the deity in the events of that day.

To bless your food or drink you may simply make the sign of the hammer over the fare. You might also recite some formula to call upon godly might and visualize or feel the might being loaded into the food or drink. Feel this might as it is ingested. Some simply sign the hammer or recite a prayer to remind themselves of the sacrality of the event.

The hammer may be signed with the hand or a hammer token. It is also common among true folk to bless the meal in the name of a particular deity, such as Frey or Nerthus, signing with a symbol appropriate to that God and to invoke that God's power. You may also give some small token portion of your food to nature or to an appropriate animal as a sacrifice. Giving it to a household pet or to a stray dog or cat can serve, if you see fit. If done properly, throwing scraps in a compost heap or into the garden could serve as a offering to the garden's wights.

Personal hygiene, if done consciously, has a great spiritual value. This is an opportunity to wash away ill-will and evil influences and to make adjustments to encourage wanted influences and moods. Washing may become an opportunity to wash away ill-will or unright thinking and ways. These are ways that do not move you toward the achievement of your goals. If you feel any illness or ill-temper, depression, and so on, you may try to wash them away with the bath or shower water. A formula such as the following may accompany this act of visualizing and feeling the disharmonious influences in your life and mood flowing down the drain.

"Water wash away all ill-will from my heart and hidge."

You can also do this washing in a water basin and then take it to a preferred place of disposal. You might then return it to the earth of your own yard and call on it later for protection.

The disposal of hair and nail pairings is also handled in a sacred manner. They are generally given back to the earth. In the Germanic mythology the earth is said to have made of the flesh of the primeval Frost Giant(Rime-Thurs), Ymir. Fingernails may be considered to be flesh. Trees were fashioned from Ymir's hair so it is appropriate to dispose of shorn hair near a tree or in a grove. In folklore Fridays are said to be auspicious days for the clipping and disposal of nails. In the Eddas carelessly discarded nail pairings are said to contribute to the forces of non-conscious chaos amassing for Ragnarök— or the final conflagration of the world.

Meditation

There are a variety of ways to meditate for those who have the time for more involved forms of prayer. Meditation can be a way of simply relaxing and centering one's self or it can involve reflection on the holy and the whole of life.

If you live a busy life that allows little or no time for private pursuits such as lengthy meditations, you can do yourself great good by finding a place to be alone for a few minutes a day to center yourself and gather your thoughts and renew energy before jumping back into the fray. If park land is available, see if you can't spend a few minutes there during a break, lunch hour or after work. Clear your head of the day's business and relax, watch and listen. Clear your head of all thought whatever for a few moments.

There are a number of relaxation and meditation techniques not directly found in Germanic sources practiced today that can be useful. Some of these are so universal as to be of general use, while others are fairly free of any cultural bias and can be freely adapted by true folk. The important thing is that you can get into a relaxed state in which you can clear your mind of its usual preoccupations to gain access to other inner resources.

Think deeply on one of the myths found in the Eddas. Think about who is doing what and why. You will likely come up with a number of questions. Look into your own life for comparable incidents and circumstances and compare the behavior of the mythic figures with those from your memory. Seek to understand the motives of the mythic figures by looking at the motives of the figures in your own memory. With this technique you will give meaning and life to the myth and it may give meaning and insight into some of the events of your own life. In this way the myth becomes linked with real life situations for you. When you are thinking about these events put yourself in the place of those you understand least. The great value of mythic events is that they are structurally archetypal. Their structures, their very forms, underlie the complex tapestry of often seemingly irrelevant events that make up our everyday lives. The better we understand these structures and the better we can recognize them in the happenings around us, the better we will be able to do right and to take effective action.

The "Hávamál" in the *Poetic Edda* is, on one level, the least metaphorical of all the Eddic poems. Much of it is straightforward advice on conducting day to day affairs. The problem for us is that this specific advice is given in a particular cultural context and we need to rethink the advice in terms of situations in the 20th and 21st centuries. If you ponder the advice of the "Hávamál" deeply, you will become adept at finding the modern equivalents to the situations and ethical problems described in the poem.

Chapter 10
LANDTAKING

This chapter is about claiming new land, leaving old property, new houses, and warding the land against unwanted influences. Whether you are moving into a new apartment for a few months, or are settling down for a lifetime, you will want to make the land and the space your own for the time of the stay.

Our most distant cultural ancestors — the semi-nomadic Indo-European tribesmen — were a migrating lot. They moved from place to place often— modern Americans are much like them in many ways. But the spiritual center of the folk — to be found ultimately not in the land but in the heart of the folk itself — is where ever the folk is at that time. The center of the world is a mobile one— this is a fact that we all somehow understand. It is inherited from our forefathers.

Viking Age sources give us the basics and folk-ways give us additional facts for the reconstruction of the landtaking ceremony of the Teutons. In Old Norse this process is known as *landnáma*. During the Viking Age fire and sacred furniture from the old dwelling were brought to the new land. The fire is borne around the perimeter of the new territory and the sacred furniture, most typically the high-seat or porch pillars, is installed at the site of the new hearth. The highest pillars seem to have been those that stood at the sides of the bench where the head of the household presided over feasts in the hall. They may have been pillars that supported the roof and the porch pillars were likely those that stood before the main entrance of the hall. These pillars may have been dedicated to deities and have been carved with sacred motifs. Some of these — especially those sacred to the God Thor — were also studded with "godly nails." You may want to carry fire from the hearth at the old dwelling to the new site to bear it abound the property in a procession and rekindle the flames of the new hearth and stall. One way to carry the flame over short distances is by means of a propane lantern or other protected and safe flame. Another option is to kindle the flames afresh at the new stead as you might rekindle the flame of the year at the Yule-tide. This would most traditionally be a need-fire generated by friction between two pieces of wood by means of a device such as a fire-drill, though this is hardly essential.

When the new fire is ready, it should be borne in a procession made up of the new inhabitants and perhaps some of their friends and family. The procession should not only go around the boundaries of the property, but should also go around the house itself— inside and outside. Apartment dwellers need only carry the fire around inside. Take special care to take the fire to the thresholds, the four most extreme corners of the dwelling and the hearth. Begin at the main threshold and end at the main threshold. Standing at the threshold the speaker may say such words as are given in *A Book of*

Troth for this occasion, or whatever words seem most right. Be sure to state your name(s) and that you have some for the purpose of taking the stead upon which you will thereafter rightly dwell.

The land may also be hallowed with the Hammer Working. While walking along each side of the land you may make the sign of the hammer and say "The hammer of Thunar (Thor) hallow this land and ward it well!" The others in the procession may respond: "By troth the land is taken and well it is warded!" Other words may be substituted, of course. If several people plan to live on the land are taking it together, the folk may station themselves at intervals and relay the fire, or take turns bearing the flame as they all proceed together.

At this time you should also make an offering to the wights that already dwell on the land, or to drive some or all of them away, if that seems needed. It is up to your own intuition, divination or feelings to determine whether there are any wights or influences lingering on the land that will be a hindrance to your goals or seem incompatible with your ways. So keep in mind that in moving you will bring some or many wights of your own and are going to introduce them to the new land, if you can.

That land-wights are brought in the heart and soul of the folk, and are not permanently planted in the rocks and soil of the physical land, is clearly shown in the history of the *landnáma* in Iceland. The immigrants (who began arriving on the largely uninhabited island around the year 870 CE) brought with them the ancient ancestral land-wights, elves and dwarves of their native lands in Scandinavia. This tells us clearly that when the European ancestors of modern Americans came to this so-called New World they too — even if unconsciously — brought their ancestral spirits with them. These dwell in, and are expressed through, the people making up the culture more than the land they live on.

In should be borne in mind that many of the wights already inhabiting the land of North America are liable to be linked to native American cultures. Some of these may be very firmly rooted in the land and it may be better to learn to live with them — to make peace between your folk-wights and those of the Amerindians — right from the start.

Standing at the main threshold of the dwelling, the speaker should take up a horn of ale and set down the fire or hand it to another celebrant. The speaker then says: "Glad greetings and hail to all you wights who dwell in this stead! We give you honor as in the days of yore. Let there be among us frith and grith, and naught of strife." Then the speaker drinks from the horn and then the other celebrants after the speaker. The horn is returned to the speaker who pours the remainder on the ground to the wights and says: "Come ye wights to get the gifts allotted to you! Bring wealth and weal, merry wit and mirth to this home!" The speaker may then conclude the rite by saying: "Now the work has been wrought, may this home and all who dwell herein know naught but good as long as the Troth has abode within!" This is the basic rite, but there are may personalized variations within the general traditional format.

Just by moving your old furniture, art and holy things, you will introduce wights from your old dwelling. Be careful to select the influences and wights you want. You may want to do some kind of banishing rite as described above to get rid of those that were hindrances. If there are objects you know are associated with unwanted wights or influences, you might want to leave them in the old house or sell them to someone else at a garage ale or give them to Goodwill. You can find the oddest things at Goodwill.

Be sure and do a blessing to the wights from the old stead that you want to cultivate in the new place as soon as possible. You may perform a blessing for each of the different kinds of wights separately and give them some area of the property to them.

To keep the harmonious influences alive in your house, you need to prevent the intrusion of disruptive influences and quickly drive away those that do get in, and inevitably they will get in, just as sure as dust and dirt. Like dust and dirt, these can be controlled by watchfulness.

To ward your stead against unwanted wights and ways, you can set charms about the extremities of the premises, especially the thresholds. Wheels and birch branches are commonly set over thresholds. You may also designate some wights as wardens and make charms calling on their might to ward the dwelling against evil. The heads of beasts, such as those found on the prows of Viking ships, may be attached to parts of the house or fences. Be careful about setting them up on poles, lest they be taken for Niding poles. Niding poles like the monstrous heads of the ship prows, had an offensive purpose well beyond protection and were used to drive away the helpful wights and luck of an enemy's hearth and homeland. The function of such images depends more on the purpose to which they are given in their initial shaping and loading than on their shapes. See chapter 19 for more on this.

Moving

When moving into a new home, it is customary to send in a pet or other animal first. This is possibly a memory of the time in which sacrifices were given to new abodes and their remains buried beneath the hearth stone. It is thought best to move into a dwelling during the waxing or full moon. Skulls and bones of horses and other animals have been excavated from beneath the hearths and foundation walls of many ancient Teutonic dwellings.

Bring salt and bread inside as you move in and you will never lack provisions and prosperity.

If you should have the rare opportunity to have your home built up on an empty lot, go out and work a blessing to the wights and pour out libations of blessing ale or beer onto the site where the foundation is to be laid. As the structure is being raised you may visit at night when the workers are away and carve spells into the timbers and put talismans behind the walls. If you don't perform a blessing, you may just pour beer or ale out onto the foundation site. In doing such a foundation rite you might include a reading and rede from the story of the founding of Asgard or another great edifice.

The first fruits of the harvest for the year, traditionally four kernels of grain, are placed in the four extreme corners of the house. Nowadays we may use coins, paper money or other tokens of our labor.

When entering a new house, say: "Luck in here!"

Chapter 11
LIFE-TIDES AND INITIATION

The rites of crossing over from one stage of life to another are an integral part of most traditional societies. The transition from one status to another involves replacing one set of thought and behavior patterns that the individual has internalized and lived by with another set of patterns more suited to another status in society. The differences can be very profound between one status and another. The consequences of failure of individuals to adjust to new social positions can have severe consequences for the person and society.

The single greatest crossing-over is that from childhood to adulthood. In our society there is no longer any significant demarcation between these two states of being. The closest thing we have to a rite of passage into adulthood is likely the high school graduation ceremony, though there are many other points prior to graduation which may also be seen as such. These include the acquisition of a driver's license, the first car, the first job, the first rifle, and so on. Unfortunately these tend to serve as a series of preparations for the final act of moving out of the parental home, and also may serve as a series of false starts in that they are not necessarily accompanied by real legal and social responsibilities. The closest thing to a primitive rite of coming to adulthood the modern American is likely to experience in mainstream culture is the Jewish *Bar Mitzvah* ceremony.

The threefold structure of the rite of passage includes a period of severance, a liminal period, and a re-entry stage. So there are rites of separation, transformation, and re-integration. Prior to the actual rite there may be a long period of preparatory instruction. In the severance phase initiates symbolically cut all ties with family and society and often symbolically die. Initiate will then ideally live apart from society in a liminal stage during which they come to terms with, and internalize, their new role in the world. A part or all of the liminal period can involve complete isolation or contact only with other initiates and adult guides or masters. With this symbolic death initiates symbolically kill what they once were, cut all ties with everything in their old lives. In the liminal phase, initiates found a new order of being and plan their future behavior, or allow their guides to do this for them. In re-entry initiates are reborn anew into the society and are from that time forward expected to act in accordance with the behaviors appropriate to their new status. They are also treated with the respect due to individuals of that status. The re-entry phase may be characterized by a declaration or purpose by the initiates and gestures of acceptance by the public.

The liminal period is a time in which all the old rules of society have disappeared and initiates live outside the bounds of society as an *outlaw*. (One outside the bounds of law or social norms.) This is the time in which initiates are instilled with a new vision and purpose. Those who isolate themselves in the wilderness may have the opportunity to escape the bonds of society in a profound way, and to listen to their inner redes. The liminal time is also a time of tests and of literal transformation. The person moves from one form of being to another. It is here guides indoctrinate initiates with the lore and secrets of their new status and test them over their knowledge and skills.

The more important life-tides, or limes of life, will be discussed in this section including the rites of birth, wedlock and death. The same principles may be applied to rites for crossing into mid-life, old age and divorce, as well as initiation into special societies and orders.

Coming into the Clan

There are four ways by which an individual becomes part of a family or clan: by birth, by marriage, by adoption, and by blood-siblinghood. As the Troth is a kind of tribal or natural folk-religion, individuals can not really be "converted" to it. They are either born to it as a part of the heritage of their blood, or they enter it by marriage, adoption or blood-siblinghood.

Birth-Rites

It is as a part of the rituals performed at the time of a child's birth that a child is given official entry into the family and society— and into the human race itself. Prior to naming, a child stands outside the pale of humanity, without a comprehensive human soul. The workings of naming are crucial to proper integration of the child into the family by ensuring the successful "ensoulment" of the child with an ancestral haming and fetch. The core traits of a child's being are determined by the ancestral soul(s) manifested during the birth process. It may be that a child is marked out for a particular soul from the moment of conception, or before. Upon naming, the child is recognized as the rebirth of a clanic ancestor from either the mother's or father's side of the family.

Before a child is even born, even before conception, it is possible to plan to encourage the rebirth of a particular ancestor. During the period of pregnancy, a family may encourage the rebirth of a particular ancestor by the retelling the person's deeds in ritual contexts, by holding memory-drinkings in the person's honor and other ritual workings. Each clan has its own traditions and ways in these matters. When a family is not set on the rebirth of a particular ancestor, or if the omens are not favorable for the rebirth of the ancestor the family is looking to have reborn, divination may be employed to discover the identity of the ancestor. Sometimes it is simply known who is going to be reborn, especially in the case of a child born after the death of its father, in which case it is quite likely that a son will be the father reborn.

To find out who is trying to be reborn in a child you might try reciting ancestral names over a child until it, or something in the immediate environment, gives a sign. In some traditional societies, ancestral names are recited over a baby and its crying tells the family when the right ancestor has been named. Even with all the workings and divination, it is still possible that the baby is given the wrong name. This will be clear when as the child grows and his behavior fails to accord with the characteristics linked to his name. In the sagas children are sometimes renamed under these circumstances. If it is not clear just who the child really is, it may be necessary to go through a divinatory process again.

In elder times, a family might consult a spæ-wife about the nature and destiny of a child. These seeresses travelled around the countryside visiting those who invited them. In the Old Norse tale *Nornagestsþáttr* (Tale of Nornagest) three women travelling together as "norns" looked into the destiny of a baby. Out of spite one of them lay a curse on the boy, though another mollified the curse. Be careful who you have around your child during its first days.

Traditionally, nine days were allowed between the time the child was born and the time it was ritually sprinkled with water and named. This is the period in which the family divines a name and decides whether the child is an appropriate vehicle for the expression of a particular ancestral soul. In pre-industrial times, this was often a time in which it was determined whether the body of the child was suited for life in Midgard. If the child was deformed or in some other way deemed ill-suited, it was exposed to the elements of nature to die. This was thought better than condemning an ancestor to the degradation of living as an invalid in a world with little room for those who could not hold their own. Nothing would be considered lost as the soul that had begun to attach itself would be freed until it was called again by another birth in the family. The rest is returned to the natural order from which it sprang. This attitude toward the sacral nature of a life of quality held by our ancestors can act as a guiding principle in certain issues facing families today— such as death with dignity, or abortion.

If the ancestor has a Germanic name, even if it is a middle name, this is the real name, and this is the name that should be a part of the child's name. Celtic names are next in order of preference, and other European names after that. A certain *harmony* between the name and the flesh and bones it designates is desirable.

The haming and the fetch are the parts of the soul that are reborn. The individual consciousness and memory do not tend to survive the transition. The memories of "past lives" are preserved by the clan and are imparted again to an individual through family tradition.

The haming and fetch become powerful as they progress through more clan lives. The haming has the experience gained from all the previous lives and harbors the vitality of all the departed. In the Viking Age one generation was expected to outdo the deeds of the previous one. It was hoped that the sons would surpass the works of their fathers. In this way the clanic haming and fetches were thought to be ever increasing in their power. In naming a soul into a child the father and mother may want to consider the kind of luck they want to bring into the family. Different names are associated with different kinds of luck and power. Some names may be connected to luck in business, others with good harvests in agriculture, and others with luck in fishing, science or mathematics. The haming of certain names may also have their own sides in certain situations, and these need to be considered.

Both to provide some suggestions for authentically Germanic, yet traditionally Anglo-Saxon, , names we have provided a list of both men's and women's names. You might also notice how many of these names are also known in their Italian and Spanish forms; for example: Adolfo, Frederico, Carlo, and so on.This is because the Goths established kingdoms in both Spain and Italy during the Migration Age (fifth to eighth centuries) and their names have become well liked in those lands.

These names can be used in selecting a name for a child, or in renaming yourself for sacred purposes. Also, it is interesting to learn the heritage of your own given name. A study of the names of our traditional ancestors gives us a vision of their values and goals in life. From these we can learn much.

Some Men's Names

Note that many of the men's names also have feminine versions, for example Carla for Carl, or Edwina for Edwin.

Adolph: "Noble Wolf"
Alaric: "All-ruler"
Albert: "Noble-bright"
Alfred: "Elf in Council"
Anselm: "Godly Helmet"
Archibald: "Nobly Bold"
Arnold: "Strong as an Eagle"
Athelstan: "Noble Stone"
Baldwin: "Bold or Courageous Friend"
Bernard: "Bold as a Bear"
Berthold: "Bright Ruler"
Bertram: "Bright Raven"
Carl/Charles: "Free-man"
Conrad: "Bold Council"
Cuthbert: "Noted Brightness"
Earl: "Noble Man"
Edgar: "Spear of Treasure"
Edmund: "Defender of the Treasure"
Edward: "Guardian of the Treasure"
Edwin: "Gainer of Treasure"
Egbert: "Bright-edge"
Eldred: "Ancient Council"
Elmer: "Famous in Nobility"

Everard: "Strong as a Boar"
Frank/Francis: "Free-man"
Frederick: "Ruling in Peace"
Gerald: "Spear-wielder"
Gerard: "Strong with a Spear"
Gilbert: "Bright Wish"
Goddard: "God-strong"
Godfrey:"Peace of God"
Godwin: "Friend of God"
Herold (Harald): "Army-leader"
Henry: "Ruler of an Enclosure"
Herbert: "Glory of the Army"
Herman: "Army-man" (warrior)
Howard: "Guardian of the Grave-mound"
Hubert: "Bright Mind"
Hugh/Hugo: "Mind"
Kenhelm: "Bold Helm"
Lambert: "Illustrious with Landed Possessions"
Leonard: "Strong as a Lion"
Leopold: "Bold for the People"
Luther: "Illustrious Warrior"
Marvin: "Sea-friend"
Norbert: "Njord's Brightness"
Norman: "North-man"
Osbert: "Godly bright"
Osmund: "Protection of God"
Raymond: "Wise Protection"
Reginald:"Strong Ruler"
Richard: "Strong like a Ruler"
Roderic: "Rich in Fame"
Roger: "Famous with the Spear"
Roland: "Famous of the Land"
Robert: "Bright in Fame"
Seward (Sigurd): "Guardian of Victory"
Sigfrid: "Peach through Victory"
Sigmund: "Protector of Victory"
Theobald: "Bold for the People"
Theoderic: "Ruler of the People"
Thurston: "Thor's Stone"
Walter: "Ruling the Army"
Wilfred: "Desire for Peace"
William: "Willful Helmet"
Winfred: "Win-peace"

Some Women's Names

Note that from these women's names it becomes clear that the ancestors had a very different view of what it was to be a "real woman" than later Christian culture would have us believe.

Adelaide: "Of Noble Rank"
Adelina: "Of Noble Birth"
Alda: "Powerful"
Alfreda: "Elven Peace"
Amelia: "Industrious"
Astrid: "Of Divine Power"
Bertha: "Bright"
Brunnhilda: "Breast-plate of Battle"
Emma: "Healer"
Erda: "Earthly"
Ethel: "Noble"
Frieda: "Peace"
Gerda: "Protected"
Gertrude: "Spear-maiden"
Hedwig: "Strife"
Helga: "Holy"
Hilda: "Battler"
Hildagard: "Enclosure of Battle"
Mathilda: "Mighty Battle-maid"
Mildred: "Gentle Council"
Millicent: Strong"
Sigrid: "victory rider"
Starr: "Star"
Swanhilda: "Swan of Battle"
Ulrica: "All-ruling"
Valda: "She who Rules"
Winifred: "Friend of Peace"
Winola: "Little Friend"
Yrsa: "She-Wolf"

There are, of course, hundreds of other names that could be given. For more you can consult a good book on the subject of given names. Unfortunately, there are very few good ones. Most are inaccurate in the "translations" they give for the names. Be sure your source is fairly recent and was written by a recognized scholar in the field of *onomastics* (the study of names).

Immediately after a child was born, it was set down on the ground to gain contact with the ultimate mother— Mother Earth (Old High German: Erda, Old Norse: Jörð). One tradition has it that a child should be placed on its right side first.

On the ninth night after birth, the mother and father and perhaps some other members of the family gather around the household stall or hearth. Ideally the shrine specially dedicated to the ancestors will also be present. If not, be certain that mementos that belonged to other ancestors who bore the name the child is about to receive are present. One of these, or another object once possessed by one of the ancestors after whom the child was named, should serve as a naming-gift. The naming-gift fixes the spiritual qualities of the name to the child.

After the recitation of some of the deeds associated with the folks after whom the child is named, the mother brings the child to the father who takes it in his arms and sets it to rest in his lap. He then sprinkles the child with pure spring water and speaks the name of the child in such words as seem right. The following quotes from Icelandic sagas tell us much about how this ritual speech sounded. "This boy shall be called Ingimund, after his mother's father and I look for luck (haming) in him because of his name." Or: "This boy shall be called Thorsteinn, and I wish that luck may go with his name." By this act the father breathes the soul into the child and the child has truly entered the clan and society as a real human being. Along with the name, the father inspires the child with luck, strength, will, character and other essential qualities linked to the name. The child might then be presented with an heirloom associated with its name to quicken the growth of the ancestral haming in the new being. In olden times a father might place a sword in a baby's hand to make it brave. Thereupon all present might hail the child by its name, perhaps repeating the words of the father. In the case of a daughter it is sometimes known that the mother will sit the child on her knee and name her. One formula connected to such a naming reads: "God make thee a good woman!" This practice is echoed in an East Anglian folk-tradition which has it that the first person to kiss a child after the parents will leave his temperament on the child.

The sharing of food is another way people may share luck and power. The sharing of food is a way to forge links between people, much as sharing food and drink with the Gods, wights and ancestors strengthens the ties between us and them. Giving a child regular human food (something other than mother's milk) is another means by which a child is established as an ensouled being who shares in the luck of the clan. In Altfrid's *Life of St. Ansgar*, a father is said to be angry when his wife bears another girl after having borne no sons. The father condemned the baby to death. He ordered the baby taken from the mother before it could have mother's milk. A neighboring woman snatched the baby from the servants who took the child and ran to her own kitchen and fed the baby some honey. When the pursuers found her the baby was licking its lips and they could not, by their heathen custom, kill it.

The importance of sharing food as a means of sharing family luck and creating a binding effect is well illustrated by the Viking Age custom of "bench-mates" (that is, those who would share a place at a bench or table in the hall of a lord) in a retinue who will their possessions to one another when they were far from family.

It is customary to give a child a gift when it teethes. Naming should always be accompanied by a gift called a name-fastener (Old Norse *nafnfestr*). The practice of the father putting a sword in a baby boy's hand to make him brave survived well beyond the Viking Age. Even those given nick-names have been known to ask for gifts of their name-givers. In the Viking Age nick-names were extremely important and worked much like sir-names do today. The nick-name highlights some distinguishing aspect of an individual character. You might have the ancestral name Ragnar and your nick-name "Ace" sets you apart from all the other Ragnars in the family line and in the town or district.

An East Anglian tradition has it that children born on the chime hours of three, six, nine or twelve will be gifted with prophetic powers.

Naming Blessing

The father of the child is seated in a chair next to the stall or harrow. The mother enters the room carrying the baby. It is most usual for the father to be the chief reader in this ceremony, but an Elder can also substitute.

1. Hallowing:

The stead is hallowed in the usual manner with a Hammer Working.

2. Reading:

Read or recite a passage on the works and virtues of the ancestors who held the name in question before the new recipient.

3. Rede:

Declare the purpose of the gathering in straightforward terms. Here is an example of how such a speech could go: "We gather here in this hallowed stead to bring this boy into the clan with the luck of the name Edward that was given to his great grandfather before him, and his great great grandfather before that. By these names and the name (here insert clanic or surname) the might and main of our holy haming shall be breathed into this boy and give him the right stuff."

4 Call:

"Hail all the high and holy Gods and Goddesses of the Æsir and Vanir! Hail the holy dises, the elves and the landwights of our folk! Hail our forefolk!" Then make a specific call to the spirit of the name and to the special talents or abilities that are to come with the name. To continue with the example, we might find:

"Hail Edward Jack Dietrick, he who founded forges and fashioned tongs! We bid thee welcome!"

In a like manner list other important ancestors, including those after whom the child is to be named. Also invite and honor any wights that are especially sacred to the clans.

5. Loading:

The holy water is charged with the might of the clan and the blessings of the Gods. A drink might also be loaded. Let the might and main of our family and the luck of our folk be in this water, and the blessings of our Gods and Goddesses, too.

6. Drinking:

If a drink has been loaded as well, then it is drunk and shared with the child.

7. Sprinkling:

The child is presented to the father by the mother. She hands the baby to him and he places it in his lap. The baby is then sprinkled on the top of the head with the holy water. As the water is sprinkled the father names the child with words such as: "I sprinkle you with water and give you the name Edward, after your great grandfather, and his father before him."

8. Blessing:

Any remaining water is poured out onto the ground or into the auxiliary bowl in the names of the powers and divinities who have been called upon in the rite.

9. Leaving:

"Thus the work is wrought, so it is done."

There are other folkish customs of heathen origin that have been practiced into the modern era. There are numerous traditions concerning the kinds of gifts given to children. Many are said to be given to help prevent the child from being made a changeling by an elf or dwarf. This is likely a reinterpretation of an old tradition in which ancestral spirits were encouraged to find their way to a child. Of course, one wants to discourage the unwanted as well as encouraging the desired influences from affecting one's child. The key is the most common gift to be bestowed on a baby and put it in its crib— usually to keep the elves and unwanted wights away. Swords and knives with their points sticking out may be put in the cradle for similar purposes. It is not always said that these things are given for any purpose other than luck. Other items may be given to influence a child's luck in specific areas of life. Ideally you should try to encourage the kinds of luck that tends to run in your family with these gifts. Pennies and other monies may be given to help ensure the child's future prosperity. Bread may be given to ensure that food will not be lacking. For this purpose you may also place such gifts in the child's first bath water. A pen may be put in its bath water to help it learn fast, and an egg will give it a clear voice. Three pennies may be put in the bath for wealth. Naturally, many other items may be given as well to affect other attributes. The bath water may be emptied under a green tree.

To bring a child health, pass it through a hole in the earth or over the hearth, the stall, or an ancestral burial place.

Numerous other customs are to be found in the records of regional European folklore. Often traditions are contradictory and given a Christian interpretation. This is to be expected due to historical circumstances. The real significance of much of this will reveal itself in time after some practical experience in the customs has been gained. Books can not teach you the true meaning of the customs— only actual practice can do that — and do it *directly*. Meanwhile, if you are partial to any particular region, say the parts of Europe from which your own ancestors came, look into the folklore of that specific region.

Chapter 12
HOLY WEDLOCK

By wedlock two clans or families may be joined together and one partner may officially become a part of the other partner's clan or family. Typically, it is the woman who joins the clan of her husband, though the man may also chose to join the woman's family. By wedlock two families or clans can be bound together to form a true tribe. In Germanic culture wedlock is a social more than legal fact. If a couple is cohabiting they are considered married regardless of the presence or absence of legal or ritual formalities. This is customary in Germanic or English "common law," hence the phrase "common law marriage."

A wedding may be celebrated in private and involve little more than the exchange of rings and the sharing of bridal ale and gifts, oaths of betrothal, and an embrace and kiss before a witness. These are the basic elements of the betrothal. Because of the profound implications of the act of wedlock for the family and friends of bother concerned, it is typical for the whole to gather to see that the binding of the couple and the two families is brought about successfully and in good cheer and good frith. A couple might celebrate both a public and private ceremony. In ancient times it was often customary to a pair to go through a betrothal ceremony and a period of betrothal before the actual marriage ceremony.

Ideally, an Elder of the Ring of Troth who is legally entitled to bind couples in marriage will be procured for a public wedding.

There are a variety of folk customs concerning the most auspicious and inauspicious times for a wedding. Judging by the many contradictory traditions it seems that it is really up to each individual family to decide according to its own needs what the time and place of the wedding should be.

Witnesses should be available to speak on behalf of both parties to vouch for their character and the nobility of their forefolks. The bride and her witnesses and family should stand to one side of the stall, while the groom and his family and witnesses stand to the other side of the stall.

The Elder then summons the Gods to witness, especially those who take a special interest in marriages such as Frigga, Lofn, Siofn, Varr Frey, Freya, Thor and the like. The Elder may single out these deities for special attention in a calling on all the wights of Asgard and Wane-Home, or may single out one or more wedding related wights in the calling.

Then the Elder calls for the witnesses to tell of the good worth of the bride. Each steps before the harrow or stall to speak and returns to his or her place. Then the groom's witnesses do the same.

A bowl of ale is then hallowed in the name of the Gods called upon and a portion is poured into a horn or another vessel from which both bride and groom drink. Remaining portions may be distributed among the gathered folk and the last poured out in honor of the Gods. As in most sacred feasts, ale is best consumed in moderation. As the High One cautions: "The best feast is that which one can remember afterwards, and recall everything that happened."

The couple then exchanges finger rings. At this moment each swears to wed and plight troth in the other. The groom might use the following words that were lawfully used in ancient Iceland: "We declare ourselves witnesses to you (here the name of the witnesses) bind me in lawful betrothal, and with taking hold of hands you promise me dowry and undertake to fulfill and observe the whole of the compact between us, which has been notified in the hearing of the witnesses without guile or cunning, as a real and authorized compact."

The groom then presents the bride with a set of keys to the household as a symbol of her dominion over domestic affairs. In many instances this may not be deemed appropriate and may be left out. In the Viking Age, when this was especially practiced, the women often ran the farms while the able bodied men were off in Viking expeditions. Nowadays both parties often share equal responsibilities in the domestic and occupational spheres.

Then the Elder hallows the wedlock by making the sign of the hammer before the couple.

They then embrace and kiss.

After the ceremony there should be a great feast at which there may be a ritual eating of a sacrificial cake of which all partake. This sacrificial cake is the origin of the importance of the modern "wedding cake" in current practice. As explained earlier, sharing food is a means by which people are bonded together. There are numerous traditions surrounding the wedding cake. The cake is in some parts of England wrapped up to be sent away to those who were unable to attend the feast. Pieces may be retained to be given back to the fields as well. For good luck nine pieces of the cake may be passed through the wedding rings.

Little is known from Viking Age sources about the proper attire for the bride and groom. The "Lay of Thrym" in the *Poetic Edda* mentions a veil and bridal linen but does not elaborate. Some of the true folk in England think red is more appropriate for weddings than white, as this is more emblematic of passionate love. This is a matter of personal choice.

Traditionally a procession forms some part of the ceremony. Usually the procession went from the house of the bride's family to that of the groom. Nowadays the procession might be from the stall before which the couple was married to the place of the reception— or the cars that take them to the reception. Here the bride and groom may be showered with grain to ensure their good luck, prosperity— and if they wish, fertility.

When the couple first arrives at their new stead, the groom carries the bride over the threshold and from there to and around the household hearth or stall.

9. Leaving:

The Elder returns to the harrow or stall and says:
"Thus the work of wedding is wrought. It renews the hearts of all who have witnessed it to be steadfast in their troth one with the other."

Chapter 13
BLOOD-BROTHER AND -SISTERHOOD

In this day and age — perhaps indeed a Wolf-Age in which the families of humanity are in widespread dissolution — there is once again need for a profound rite used in ancient times in such times of social and personal stress. A Wolf-Age is one in which the social order of humanity breaks down and a new order based on voluntary associations is called for. The old human order is replaced by a wolfish one. The way to do this has traditionally been through rites of blood-siblinghood. But it is also even more usually undertaken on private levels by two or more individuals who wish to bind themselves together in ways as tight or even tighter than if they were genetically related to one another. If the heads of clans or families do this, it is a way of binding two whole clans together— which forms the basis for a new tribe of people.

What was done regularly in ancient times perhaps needs to be reinstituted today: the binding of families and clans into new tribal organizations. Some of the most important of the old Germanic tribes, for example the Saxons (who were eventually to be the major tribe settling in England) and Franks (who were to establish the nation of France) were the result of such "artificial" tribal creations. By the way, the emblems of these two tribes, a short single-edged sword (sax) and a kind of short spear (frank) were the symbols of these new tribes because these were their favorite weapons.

So two clans may be brought together by the rite of blood-siblinghood. In this rite two people may join families and share clanic haming and obligations. The two siblings have the same obligations towards one another as those born as natural siblings.

In the Viking Age a long piece of turf was cut and raised with a spear to form an arched loop, under which the siblings were to be joined. They go to their knees and spill some of their blood into the ground and mix it with the earth. They call on the Gods to witness and then clasp hands, state the terms of the oath and swear to them.

A modern rite might involve a pit in the ground with walls built up out of the excavated earth and perhaps roofed with a piece of wood covered with earth. The essential idea is that the siblings are reborn from the womb of the same mother— Mother Earth. It seems that blood siblinghood was more often undertaken for the purpose of bonding the siblings together for the purpose of instilling trust and loyalty in the face of difficult cooperative undertakings such as Viking expeditions.

In this day and Age it is not wise to mix blood with another human being. In any event, this was not necessary in the ancient rite. Both participants blood was mixed with the Earth— which gave birth to each of them anew. In this way they were true brothers, born of the same Mother.

Few words need to be spoken for the completion of such a rite.

It is up to individuals and groups to do more practical experimentation in this area of work. Results will prove themselves. But it seems that in this new Wolf-Age there is a need for ties of new blood which will replace the old ties which are in many ways dissolving.

Chapter 14
FOSTERAGE

Adoption is another means by which an outsider may become a member of a family. Here the adopted child is brought into the family so as to share fully in its frith, luck, honor, memory and *ørlög* (or "fate"). The adopted son or daughter is for all intents and purposes a true son or daughter. As a part of a new clan, the adopted child acquires a new being as it is inspired with the haming of the new family._

The focal act of a Germanic adoption rite is the setting of the child upon the knee of the new father. In medieval Norway it was customary for the adopting family to slaughter an ox and make a boot from its hide. At a sacrificial feast at which the ox was eaten, the boot was set prominently in the main part of the room. The members of the family would then step into the boot one after the other. The adopting father would go first and the adopted son after, then the remaining family members would follow. The adopting father confirmed that the child was now family with the words: "I lead this man to the goods I gave him, to gift and repayment, to chair and seat, to fine and rings, to a full man's right, as if his mother had been bought with a bridal gift."

Another formula for adoption ceremony that has come down to us reads: "We take him into the clan with us." It was customary for the whole family to be present to confirm an adoption and it was expected that the child would be infused with haming from both the father's and the mother's family as a result of the ceremonial working.

In a modern context, the child might be placed in the father's lap in the case of a small child, but an older child might step into a special shoe. A family feast should take place shortly after the working. The child should also be given significant gift during the working or the feast.

Another model for an adoption is provided in the Salic Law code of the early 6th century. This was a code of law among the Franks along the Rhine river. The father and son come together before three witnesses and two local officials, one of whom is known as a Thunginus because his function is related to that of the "Thing" or legislative assembly. The three witnesses ask the father one question each and the man throws a staff into the lap of the lad and states the amount of property the boy is to inherit and how he is to get it. Then the witnesses visit the man at his home to see that the man does in fact have as much property. It is important that the witnesses be treated as guests and fed. After that the father must go before a regional or royal court and proclaim the terms of inheritance before a royal official. The three witnesses will be required to testify as to the term of the agreement if the arrangement is ever contested. If a boy is to be an heir then the modern adoption rite should include the giving of a staff that symbolizes authority over some of the property of the father as one of the gifts of adoption.

In this, as in so much else in Germanic ritual and religious custom, we find the sacred significance of *witnesses* who make ritual or symbolic actions objectively real in the social world, and of *finances* which make such actions objectively real in the economic world.

Chapter 15
WAKES AND GRAVE

Cremation was more prominent in traditional European society than it is now, but burial was common also. Whether a body was burned or buried, the remains would be usually be interred in a mound along with certain possessions.

Wakes and proper burial practices ensure that the parts of the soul of the deceased find their appropriate places in the nine worlds. The success of the burial rites is essential to the health and luck of the clan— the haming and luck and fetch(es) of powerful persons need to be reborn in the clan. The haming provides the basic numinous power. The fetch provides a link with the ancestral memory whereby the intellect and other elements of the character of the departed ma be regenerated.

The lykes can either be interred whole, or incinerated. Burning is most appropriate for devotees of Æsiric Gods while burial is most appropriate for devotees of Vanic Gods and Goddesses. In either case the remains are interred and some kind of marker is erected such as a mound or a runestone or both. It is ideal if the remains can be interred on family property or in proximity to the graves of other family members.

The dead should be buried with some of the things or types of things that were especially important to him or her during life. One such thing might be an heirloom associated with the name of the deceased. Such heirlooms would be disintered when the name of the dead person is again given to a newborn member of the family. The object is then given as a gift to the child receiving the name. This facilitates the transference of the haming connected with the name to the child who receives the name and fastens it to the child.

Along with these kind of goods, objects associated with sustenance in daily life such as eating and drinking vessels, drink, and grain, can also be interred.

If a runic monument is to be carved, you might write to the Ring of Troth or the Rune-Gild to see if you can get an Elder or Drighten to execute the carvings. The stone should be erected between nine months and a year after the death. There are many stones standing today to draw upon for models. An Odian might consider having a stone monument modelled after any number of runestone styles, including the pictorial style of the Gotland stones which show scenes of the dead arriving in Valhalla greeted by valkyrie and arriving on Sleipnir. Likewise, you might see about getting an Elder or Drighten to perform the funeral rites, though these can be performed by a member of the family as well. It is most traditional for a son to perform the funeral rites for his father— just as the father had performed the birth rites for his son.

The funeral itself should follow shortly after death. Funerals consist of five basic parts: 1) Hallowing, 2) Call to the Gods, Goddesses and ancestors, 3) Sending the dead on their journey, 4) drinking the myne-horn in honor of the departed's memory much as one would drink to an ancestor in a sumble, 5) leaving, in which all bid the departed farewell.

The funeral ceremony itself might be followed by a wake (a ritual ale drinking) in honor of the departed. The wake is comprised of a feast, perhaps some ritual games, and a myne-drinking in honor of the departed. Here a skald or musician may recite poems or songs recounting the worthy deeds of the deceased. The closest relatives, on, fathers, mother, daughter, and so on, are expected to make the main contributions. In large wakes it may be that only the close relatives make toasts at the sumble.

For interment, the lyke is dressed in its finest clothing, including jewelry and a pocket full of cash, credit card, checkbook and other symbols of wealth. Corpse and ashes are typically interred in some form of vehicle, symbolic or real. Coffins may be made from canoes, rafts, small row boats, cars, carts, wagons, and so forth. If the actual vehicle is not included, a set of keys may be. It i also traditional to shape a grave like a small Viking-style ship. This may be done by building up a mound or by surrounding the grave with stone markers that create a configuration shaped like a ship.

Ashes are typically interred in urns made up of soapstone, clay, earthenware, wood and iron.

In some regions it is customary to carry a newly dead body three times around its house. In the Viking Age it was common to perform a Nabiargir on a newly dead corpse. In this ritual action the eyelids and nostrils were pressed closed to prevent misfortunes from occurring to those who come into the presence of the corpse. If someone dies in the household it was customary to take them out over the threshold head first in some regions. Sometime it was thought it best to remove the dead through a window rather than take them over the threshold at all. A 9th century manual of what Christian sinners must do to atone their sins (a penitential) warns against burning grain for the dead. This was presumably done at other times than the burial itself. You might also set an image of a dove on a pole and point it in the direction in which the departed died.

After the ceremonies, some mementos may be given out to close or interested relatives to set on their family shrines.

Part III
Holy Steads

Chapter 16
THE THRESHOLD

The threshold is the gateway between your household and the outer world or the community as a whole. Behind the threshold lies the haven of your hearth, an island of your own personal space. Threshold magic is used to ward the sanctuary of the hearth against unwanted "influences," "spirits" and other invasions of our spiritual sanctuary. At the same time it is used to make wanted influences welcome. Threshold magic is also used to aid in the transition between public and private domains. In a like manner, threshold magic is used to mark off one room from another. In the true household, each room is set apart from the others by its own mood or "spiritual energy" that helps generate appropriate states of mind in those who enter the room or space. When you enter your garage, the magic of the threshold helps you to cast off all distracting thoughts you might have with the activities of the study or other rooms. Effective transitions like this will help you to "get into" the activities of a given room and to do them with heart, to do them well, to do them in a sacred manner.

The threshold between the inner sanctuary of the household and the world of the community is perhaps the most important. Whenever you have some trouble getting across your threshold as you leave, especially as you leave to engage in some important business, such as going to a day's work, it is a sign that you may not be making a good transition into the proper state of mind or that some trouble may indeed lurk ahead. If you should trip, stub your toe, or your clothing gets caught on the way out, step back into the house and rest for a few minutes. Get composed, remind yourself of the activities that lie ahead and the kind of spiritual energies and resources that you will need to summon. Look upon any symbols you might have hanging on or around the threshold that are meant to facilitate your transition to the proper frame of mind and regain your composure.

The exact kinds of symbols you set on or by your threshold will depend on your own temperament and occupations.

Charms set outside can be used to facilitate the transition into the household mode, but are most especially designed to protect the premises and to encourage the presence of friendly wights and feelings. Common charms for this purpose include setting a birch branch over the door to keep away the effects of ill-will from without. Jagged lines, like lightening strokes or *sowilo*-runes, may be carved over the threshold, on or above the lintel, to prevent destruction by lightening or fire according to modern practitioners of the tradition. Likewise carving or placing a cross with four dots .+. over the door or in the door jamb may be used to promote good luck. Eight or six spoked wheels are also hung over thresholds for this purpose. Symbols of family luck or haming or so-called Pennsylvania Dutch hex-signs may also be set out to promote luck and prosperity. (An example of a Dutch hex-sign can be seen in figure 16.1.)

Figure 16.1: A Dutch Hex-Sign for Prosperity

On nights when ancestral spirits are thought to roam the world in abundance — due to a thinning of the walls between the worlds of the folks of Midgard and the realm of various kinds of ancestral spirits, including elves and trolls — sun wheels may be scratched on the doors to keep away unwanted visitors. You may also want to set a place at the table for, and formally invite in, the ancestral spirits of your own clan.

To help make the transition between one mode and another, you might set some symbol or some words of wisdom on or over the door. If you choose a quotation from the "Hávamál" to post on or near a doorway, you might recite it out loud while thinking on the doings that lie ahead. Especially recall the feelings you get when you are doing these activities well. Eventually, you will generate this state of mind simply by entering the room with the intent to engage in certain activities. The way you furnish and decorate a room will have much to do with the mood of a room.

The main threshold, whether your front door or the gate to your yard, may be used to symbolize greater thresholds and transitions, such as that between times of the year and the tides of life. The main gate may be altered for special occasions such as weddings, funerals, seasonal festivals and other rites of passage. Processions may be made through the gate to pass from one state to another symbolically. When you are about to embark on a new project, you might wrap a tool or object associated with the project in linen and set it on the threshold and walk or drive over it. Linen is a magical symbol of vitality and increase in power. Wrapping an object with it and making progress over it charges the symbol of that action with increase and dynamism.

An old English custom has it that if you forget what you are going to say, you can step over the threshold of the house and you will be able to recall it.

Thresholds are the symbolic gateways between the spiritual world of one room and another, and the magic of each doorway should facilitate the transition between and among the various modes of being and acting represented by the different rooms in any given house.

Chapter 17
HOUSEHOLD STALLS

The household stall (or altar) is the most important single site for an individual's daily and nightly observation of the Troth. It is that place in the house where the spiritual force of the Gods, ancestors, and of the living family members is focused. It acts as a kind of window or doorway to the world of the ancestors and Gods, as well as a point for the spirits of the living family members to meet and mingle. The stall becomes the living, active embodiment of the clan (or tribe) linking the past with the present, and bringing together all elements of the present to forge a strong link with that which is yet to be.

The national religion of Japan, Shinto, has sometimes been called the "sister religion" of the Troth. This is quite apt, as both are ancestral religions. In the typical Japanese household there may be one or two shrines. One usually Shinto in nature, the other Buddhist. The Japanese have no problem in being both Shinto and Buddhist. We suspect that many Trothers will now and in the future find themselves adherents of more than one religion as well. The Shinto shrine consists of a shelf (*kami-dana*) upon which a miniature version of a shrine is placed. In front there is often a small mirror, on either side of which are small lanterns and a sprig of *sakaki*. Above and across the shrine is a straw rope with talismanic paper pendants. Inside the miniature shrine is a talisman of the Grand Shrine of Ise. Also included in the shrine are talismans of various *kami* (divine beings). There may also be a separate shelf for the talismans of ancestral spirits. The average Japanese Shintoist may pay little attention to the shrine on a daily basis, but it is maintained with dignity, and is visited on solemn occasions. The more pious Japanese will pay a daily visit to the shrine and make simple observances, perhaps making offerings of rice cakes.

Now and in the future the average Trother may also pay little regular attention to the family stall— this is a shame, but it is realistic. The ancestors and Gods have so much to offer us— we should at least acknowledge this debt on a regular basis. As the ancient Hindus say: "The man who does not sacrifice is a thief!" This is because the Gods give and give, and if we do not give in return, we are stealing from them. Also, if we do not repay them for their gifts, their blessings become more and more diminished. Not necessarily because they want to give s less— but simply because they have less to give if we do not repay them.

The purpose of the stall is to be a platform for the regular display and arrangement of objects symbolic of the family's link with its ancestry and with the Gods, and to act as a focal point for regular daily and seasonal religious observances. It is a symbolic synthesis of the official sacred stall and the household hearth. The stall is usually placed in the living room of a house, but it can be placed in any room of the house which seems appropriate (except a bathroom). If you are a lone Trother living in an untrue household, set the stall up in your own room. By setting up a stall and working before it regularly you will dramatically show the virtuous nature of the Troth to all who would observe you.

A typical design for a stall is shown in figure 17.1. It is preferable to construct the stall out of wood, although any substance will do. The stall may be little more than a table or cabinet in appearance, but it should be a permanent feature of the room it is designed for, not something that is put up and taken down for certain occasions. The stall may be as large, or as small as you wish. Its dimensions really depend on the size of the room, and the number of objects it is to hold. The stall should be able to hold a drinking horn (or cup), a blessing bowl, a sprig of evergreen, and a vessel of liquid used in the rites. Mementos of the ancestors can be kept out on the top of the stall, at the back of it on the wall, or some of them may even be kept inside the stall. Images or symbols of the Gods and Goddesses especially revered by the family should appear at the back of the stall.

Figure 17.1: Typical Design of a Stall

An elaborate design for a household stall is shown in figure 17.2. This is more the type of design one might expect to find as a part of a Hof, or place of official worship in the Ring of Troth. There is no "official" set-up for such a stall— each Hof, each Garth, and each Hearth will have a slightly different version. The design of the stall will also be seen to change as the family grows in knowledge of the Troth.

Figure 17.2: Elaborate Stall Design

Working with the Stall

Before you use the stall for the first time it should be made holy, or consecrated, for its intended purpose. To do this, you should perform a general blessing for all the Gods and your ancestors. Also, during the working portion of the blessing rite, you should bring a flame from the hearth (stove, fireplace, or some other symbol of the hearth fire) and light a lamp or candle on the stall. This effectively unifies the symbol of the stall and the hearth. From that moment on the stall functions as the sacred heart and center of the spiritual life of the family or group living in that house or apartment.

From that time on it is your sacred duty to keep the stall clean and well attended. The most dutiful and true will pay a visit to the stall on a daily basis— some even go three or four times a day— upon rising, at noon, at sunset and just before going to bed. Silent meditation before the stall is all that is necessary, although some may make small offerings of grain or baked goods. These are left for a twenty-four hour period and then fed to the household animals or to the wild animals (such as birds) outside the house.

If you are fortunate enough to have an Elder of the Ring of Troth in your area who is holding the Great Blessings of the year at his or her Hof, then you should certainly attend those. However, if your Hearth or Garth live away from a working Hof, the stall (or outdoor harrow as discussed in the next chapter) becomes the focus of the regular observance of the blessings of the year. The blessing formulas given in *A Book of Troth* can be employed directly or modified for the individual use of the Hearth or Garth. The formulas used for *A Book of Troth* are those taken from the Viking Age sources we have. There are no older complete descriptions of just how Germanic folk celebrated their blessings— so these formulas have been taken as the only authentic sources we have. From these authentic sources, however, the individual or Hearth or Garth members are certainly free to improvise and innovate. But we would recommend that you try the authenticated formulas first and give them a chance to speak to you directly.

Chapter 18
YARD AND GARDEN

Many suburbanites and folks living in rural areas, of course, have some open land around their houses— even if it is only a small patch of grass behind their condos. In this space a true harrow, or outdoor altar, can be set up. The harrow is an altar usually made of stone or some other mineral substance— although a wooden structure can also be pressed into service here as well. For the most part the harrow functions as an outdoor version of the stall. However, the harrow is not as elaborate and does not have to be fitted out and maintained in the same way the stall does. The harrow is mainly used for seasonal blessings— especially those falling in the summer half of the year (from Easter through Harvest). But it is also a place where you can go outdoors to commune with the forces of nature under the open sky in a holy enclosure.

In physical appearance the harrow can be a pile of stones or bricks (about 3-4' high) with a flat top suitable for acting as an altar. A barbecue pit or structure modeled on such an object is ideal for more elaborate versions of the harrow. A typical design is shown in figure 18.1.

Figure 18.1: Typical Harrow Design

Before you use the harrow for the first time it should be made holy, or consecrated, for its intended purpose. To do this, you should perform a general blessing for all the Gods and your ancestors of the kind you would perform to consecrate a stall indoors. From the time of the consecration on the harrow functions as the sacred link of the spiritual life of the group with the outer world of the Gods and wights of nature.

Those not blessed with land of their own may find a public park, in or out of town, or some other convenient patch of nature for a brief reconnection with the land and its wights. Such moments offer a respite from the pressures and preoccupations of the daily routine and renew a sense of vitality. For some, natural settings are gateways to profound states of transcendence and communion with wights and influences of the land. This seems to have been the case with the early Germans who found powerful and direct contact with the holy in all of nature which surrounded them, finding trees, groves and springs especially vibrant channels to numinous power. According to the Roman historian Tacitus, the early Germans found their temples in groves and at springs and not in artificial enclosures. Certain groves and other natural sites were marked off as holy, but they did not surround them with walls or cover them with roofs.

If your sacred natural setting is on public land, then you may have picnics and blessings in the park though you must be careful to observe park policies. If you have your own land, you are freer to modify the landscape and to hold blessings and feasts as you please without interference from park authorities and strangers. If you do not have outdoor land you may cultivate plants indoors.

Groves

The tree is perhaps the single most holy symbol for the Germanic peoples. The tree is the primary symbol for the cosmos and the soul. A cursory reading of my book *Grove and Gallows* — a collection of Greek and Roman texts relating to Germanic religion — reveals the all-pervasiveness of the grove and sacred trees in the worship of the holy. In the 8th century the Irminsûl at Eresberg and the Great Oak of Geismar — both sites in northern Germany — stood as centers for Germanic religious worship in the face of repression. The Irminsûl may have been a great log stripped of its bark and branches, like a May-Pole, but the Oak of Geismar was a living giant of great antiquity. Trees and groves are the most natural sites for harrows and trees can serve as harrows themselves. If you are blessed with trees in your yard, then you can designate a tree as the focus of outdoor worship.

Memories of sacrificial practices in which trees serve as harrows are still to be found in European folk-ways and documented in some medieval sources. The ancient blessing typically involved a giving of both food and drink. The drink was typically poured from the blessing bowl over the roots of the tree and the food was set in the forks of the boughs or hung in the branches.

Apple trees are still wassailed in some parts of England with both a bowl of spiced cider and then cakes are set in the branches and the liquid contents of the bowl are poured over the roots. Processions and round dances are traditionally performed around trees and columns, especially during spring festivals. Gifts may also be buried near or among the roots of a holy tree.

Gardens

The folk-ways once applied to the fields are now rightly worked in the garden. The garden may now be as much an ornament as a source of sustenance, but is nevertheless rightly treated as your field even if your harvest is only in the beauty of the garden itself. The field, like the tree and well, is a cosmic symbol: the field symbolizes generative and sustaining powers of Mother Earth and the rites of the field are mainly seasonal. The folk-ways concerning the fields are perhaps the most numerous in the lore and then to hang on in history much longer than other kinds of rites.

To ensure the fertility of a field, make a procession around it in early May. You might stop at the main boundary markers and flail them with sticks in order to wake them up. This is known as "beating the bounds" in English custom. If you do not have a field or garden, you might simply walk around your yard or the inside of your apartment. It is appropriate on this occasion to carry holy relics, which include sacred images, with you around the fields. It is highly traditional to draw an image of the Earth Mother, or perhaps a May-Queen or May-Lord, around the fields in a cart or wagon. Such deities often looked after the land of an entire community or several.

In the 1st century CE the Earth Goddess, Nerthus, was drawn yearly through the fields of several Teutonic tribes in what is now northern Germany and Denmark. Images of Frey, the Lord, were borne out in a similar manner during the Viking Age in Sweden. Such images were accompanied by priests or priestesses who looked after them full-time. The priestesses who accompanied Frey's image were said to be married to the God.

At some point the fields and the Gods and wights of the fields should be blessed with givings of cakes and ale. Gifts should be made throughout the year at the outdoor shrine on appropriate occasions, such as spring and summer blessings which are often celebrated outdoors. If you know a newly married couple, have them run barefoot across the soil of your garden.

The last sheaf from the harvest is typically kept until the next year and is often made into an anthropomorphic or abstract shape called a "corn dolly" and given a name or title such as the Old Woman.

The herbs and plants form your garden may be used in sacred cooking and magical work. Leeks and onions are of special worth for magic in the Germanic tradition.

Periodically, it is good to honor your source of water. In earlier times wells and springs were given gifts and decorated. Nowadays a faucet or water cooler may serve as a well. Though gifts cannot be thrown into these sources of water, such offerings may be buried nearby. Gifts have traditionally included money, weapons and certain parts of sacrificial animals. Often these were the spoils of battle. Today offerings of money and the cakes and ale blessings are given to holy waters. Often gifts are given in exchange for wishes. Our wishing well customs and beliefs are perfectly heathen. When you see all those pennies and other coins in the tacky little fountains in the neighborhood mall— you are seeing the continuance of perfect heathen practice. We still do these things— we just often don't know why.

Waters drawn from sacred springs on Easter and on Yule even are especially holy and used in sprinklings, healings, in blessings and for magical workings.

Wells are often the sites of outdoor shrines and are linked with water wights such as Fossegrim and other kinds of trolls. These wights may be honored in blessings at the well.

Holy wells are "dressed" or "decked" (covered) annually in "Well-Dressing" ceremonies. The exterior of the wells or pump houses are decked with flowers, garlands, and green branches and/or brightly colored pieces of cloth. Wells are also decked with mythological scenes and heathen symbols created on shallow wooded trays covered with wet clay into which a mosaic made up of leaves, flower petals, pine cones and rocks, seeds, berries and other such things, is created.

Chapter 19
ART IN THE HEARTH

Art and furnishings play a powerful role in shaping the moods and energies of your places of rest, work and worship.

By means of art and furnishings, more than anything else, you can set the mood of a room. In this chapter we will look at general principles. We will discuss types of styles and the initiation of new styles and then we will consider appropriate means of depicting Gods, Goddesses and mythic scenes. In the chapters on individual areas of the house we will explore ways in which furnishings and mythic themes may be orchestrated for a powerful and resonant effect.

For the first couple of millennia of the development of northern European art, it was generally non-representational. That is to say, it was not intended to represent things in the natural world— or at least to represent them as they were actually *seen* in the natural world. It was rather to create moods and feelings in the viewer, much as music might do. This is not to say that the art was purely "decorative" and without meaning, or that it was not intended to echo phenomena in the objective world. The art was simply highly abstract and symbolic. *The study of the meaning of the images* (called iconography by art historians) of ancient European art forms is still wide open. There are very few scholars and even fewer Trothers who are seriously investigating the iconography of our ancient symbols. In judging abstract art, meanings that can be put into words or intellectualized are of secondary importance, since the real meaning is beyond the capacity of ordinary speech and speech-based thought patterns to convey. The meaning lies in the deeper realms of inner experience. Any intellectualized meaning is only valuable insofar as it helps viewers get in touch with transcendent archetypal realms of their own, and with collective, inner knowledge. It might be said that abstract Germanic art functions much as poetry, myth and ritual in helping us to sink back to our roots, down into the wells of ancestral and archetypal memory— into the Well of Mimir.

In the first millennium BCE the people of northern Europe began to bring their abstractions closer in appearance to the natural world. They did this with the use of animal ornament in which the knotwork and interlace was made up of interweaving serpentine beasts.

During the first century CE the Roman historian Tacitus (*Germania* ch. 9) reported that the Germans did not keep images of their deities in sanctuaries, although he did mention some sort of cult effigy or object carried around the countryside in a wagon in the worship of an Earth Goddess, Nerthus. On the other hand, early and late medieval Church sources, as well as various Viking Age sources, are full of references to the statues of the Gods and other sacred images.

Ultimately, the individual true family is free to use what ever style of representation they wish in the creation of objects to be the center of worship. These will range from highly abstract forms to very naturalistic ones. There are certain attributes characteristic of each of the high Gods and Goddesses which should be of some help in creating your authentic, yet individualized, depiction of the deities worshiped at your stall or harrow. Let tradition be your guide, but individual inspiration be your rule.

Here are some traditional hints for the iconography pertinent to each of the deities:

Frey

According to Adam of Bremen (a Churchman), the statue of Frey at Uppsala was endowed with a huge phallus. There is a small bronze example of such a figure found in Rällinge, Sweden. Frey, like his sister Freya, is associated with the boar. This animal and the horse are his sacrificial animals. The boar, or its tusk, may serve as a symbol for Frey. Frey is said to ride a boar named Gullinbursti ("gold-bristle"), or in a chariot drawn by this mythic animal. It too is said to have been fashioned out of gold by the dwarves— that is by artifice. Frey is sometimes also linked with cattle, an archaic symbol of wealth. All conventional symbols of wealth may be associated with an image of Frey. Frey may also be depicted with an antler, since he is said to fight the arch-giant, Surt ("the Black-One") with one at the end of times.

Freya

Freya is known for her exquisite beauty and the Brising necklace or girdle (or belt). Any image of Freya should emphasize these attributes. The presence of cats or a she-boar are also distinguishing features of this Goddess. The cats and boars the ancients had in mind were much more fierce creatures than the domesticated versions of these animals, by the way. Freya might also be pictured presiding over a hall of warriors much as Odin rule in Valhalla. This is because she takes half the battle dead to herself in her hall called Folkvang ("Plain of the Warband"). Freya should look as seductive as possible. Folkvang should appear very luxurious.

Thor

Thor is characterized most prominently by his hammer, Miöllnir. Other features include a red beard and sharp or flashing eyes. Besides his hammer, he may be depicted with gloves and a belt. He is sometimes known to ride in a wagon or chariot drawn by two goats. The goat is Thor's sacrificial animal. Great works depicting Thor in modern times include Henri Fuseli's depiction of him and the Midgard-Serpent and Arbo's painting of Thor riding his chariot through the clouds bashing etins. The hammer and thurs-runes may serve as abstract symbols of Thor. The fylfot (卐) or swastika may serve as a symbol of the hammer as well as a symbol of the sun.

Odin

Odin may appear in a number of different guises but there are a number of features which set him apart. Odin carries a spear called Gungnir and usually has a gray beard. He has one eye and may wear a broad-brimmed hat and a blue or black cloak. He may be accompanied by the ravens Hugin ("Mind") and Munin ("Memory") and by two wolves Geri ("Greedy") and Freki ("Ravenous"). Also he might be seen on his eight-legged steed called Sleipnir ("Slipper"). The ring Draupnir ("Dripper") might also be prominent. This may be interpreted as a oath ring which is typically large enough to be worn on the arm. An eagle is another symbol of Odin. Odin might also appear in the company of valkyries or wild hunters. Nooses, fetters, knots and the valknut ("knot of the fallen") are powerful symbols associated with this God. The eye — which he sacrificed for a drink of wisdom — is also a symbol of Odin. Some say the northern star is the stead of Odin's all-seeing eye.

Heimdall

Heimdall is the watchman of the Gods and may be recognized by the Giallarhorn, a huge horn by which he awakens the inhabitants of Asgard in times of danger and through which he listens for approaching danger in the meantime. Heimdall is said to have taken the form of a seal when he fought with Loki for the Brising necklace, which Loki had stolen from Freya. His hall or guard-house stands at the head of the rainbow bridge Bifröst ("Quivering-Roadway"). There he sits drinking mead. Note that in the "Völuspá" the Giallarhorn is said to rest at Mimir's well, the well of memory, a well of mead beneath the root of the world tree.

Niord

Niord is another God of wealth. He is a God more specifically of ships and cargo, as well as abundance gathered from the sea or lakes. No cult statues of Niord have been described. All we know for sure about his appearance is that his feet are much more handsome than those of the other Gods— and more so than the rest of his own body. Niord might be decked out in naval vestments. Since he is the father of Frey and Freya, he might be depicted as rather mature, perhaps with a white beard.

Idunna

She is identified by the apples she has in her care. These are the apples of eternal vitality. These may be stored in a wooden chest. An apple leaf or an apple tree might also serve as her symbols. A nut might also be seen as a sign of Idunna. The Skáldskapamál section of the *Prose Edda* tells the myth of Loki luring Idunna out of Asgard with her apples where she is snatched up by the etin named Thiassi and take to Etin-Home. In the absence of Idunna and her apples the Gods begin to grow old. So Loki is ordered to go and fetch her back. For this he needed Freya's falcon shape. He uses this to fly to Etin-Home and there turns Idunna into a nut and brings her back to Asgard in that form.

Sif

The most remarkable visible feature of Sif is her long golden hair which is said to have been fashioned by the dwarves.

Tyr

Tyr is easily recognized by his missing right hand or arm. The Tyr-rune may serve as an abstract symbol for Tyr— as his name is identical with that of the rune. Modern legal symbols may occur in the context of a work of art about Tyr. Tyr, like Odin and Thor, might also be seen to bear an oath ring.

Styles of Art

Style is the look of an art object. The style itself can communicate as much as the content (subject matter) itself. The same subject matter can tell a thousand different stories depending on the artist's interpretation. High western art, as defined by the Renaissance masters, is classical or Mediterranean in style. The classical approach regards simplicity, clarity, symmetry, balance, narrative content (it has to tell a story) as the hallmarks of fine art. Almost all of our western representational art is rooted primarily in the classical approach. The northern approach is much more abstract.

The artist who would create holy Germanic art for this new phase of the Troth has a number of options open. There are a number of German Romantics who painted scenes of Teutonic mythology. Their works may serve as models and inspiration for those who wish to work in a highly naturalistic (realistic) representational style which depict real things from the objective world.

Another approach is to look for inspiration from rich non-representational and abstract methods of heathen European art. The new art of the Troth will bring life the ancient European tradition and pick up where it left off and fuse it with the many classical permutations of the Germanic artistic spirit. Sculptors in the 20th century such as Lipchitz, Archipenko, Boccioni and Arne Vinje Gunnerud may provide models for abstractions in the shaping of godly images today.

Some of the images used today are basically wooden logs with faces and other distinctive features carved into the surface or added on. In some cases the heads are practically in the round, while some others it is almost in relief.

Those who wish to carve images, or to create traditionally based art for other purposes may want to investigate the art styles of the ancient Germans. Roger Hinks gives a good summary of the principles that characterize northern European art and set it apart from other art styles. He especially shows how it differs from the Mediterranean or classical approaches to form.

These northern tendencies continued to exert themselves in the northern way even after the conversion to Christianity with its attempt to repress the native northern culture.

These stylistic tendencies seem to exert their influence most powerfully at times when the northern countries are most independent of their southern neighbors. More detailed and definitive discussions or northern art styles are found in the works of Adama van Scheltema and Heinrich Wolflinn. In these books you will find the greatest quantity of detailed depictions of Migration Age (from around 400 to 800 CE) art objects. You might also look at *Viking Art* by Klindt Wilson. *The Sutton Hoo Ship Burial* contains good photographs of some fine Anglo-Saxon jewelry.

Those who want to look to more modern approaches would do well to study German Romanticism and Expressionism. Some excellent photographs of Romantic and other modern works that depict Germanic heathen cultural themes are to be found in *The Northern World* edited by David M. Wilson.

Some of the artists who have treated northern cultural themes include: August Malmström, Constantin Hansen, Christoffer Wilhelm Ecksberg, Peter Nicolai Arbo, Erik Werenskiold, Edward Burne-Jones, Daniel Maclise, Thomas Bruun, Johannes Flintoe, Henri Fuseli, Peter Corneleius, Axel Revold, N. A. Abilgaard, M. E. Winge, Arthur Rackham and Nils Bloommer.

You can try to get copies of artistic works, you can have them done by current artists, or, best of all, you can make them yourself. For sacred purposes often things made by one's own hand have special power and meaning.

There are several approaches to style and content of art. The naturalizing classical approach is excellent for creating scenes of historical and mythic episodes. The abstract styles are especially well suited for images and decoration to be used in holy places. Historical painting is good for reminding us of the heroic deeds of the ancestors and the noble qualities and goals for which our Gods and Goddesses stand and the way in which their powers enter our hearts and lives.

Abstract art is good for creating introspective states in which our souls may get in touch with non-ordinary moods and memories. These non-ordinary memories may be the sort of thing you would otherwise only experience or remember in a dream state. Perhaps you would never be aware of them at all. Besides creating a profound sense of awe, knowledge of these beauties and wonders can give you insight into the way these moods, though unrecognized, have a deep influence on the workings of our souls and the world. These feelings and moods, once made conscious, may be incorporated into our waking lives and drawn upon for insight, creativity, and strength of soul. For this reason, abstract forms seem especially appropriate for places of meditation, worship and magical working.

When furnishing your house with art, furniture, plants and so on, try to coordinate them so that they all contribute to the over all desired effect. The hardest part of this will certainly be deciding exactly what mood you want to encourage in a given room. You will have to consider the type of activities you want to foster in a given space. More than likely, this is predetermined for you by previous habit. You need then to determine which activity or activities you want to encourage most in the various rooms of your house. Possibly in taking such an inventory you will discover that you will want to re-assign certain activities. Most people will have special spaces assigned to cooking, to sleeping, for eating, and for socializing. If you are a student, or have children living with you who are, you might want special areas for study and perhaps also special areas for recreation. Some will have special work spaces for pursuing arts, crafts, other hobbies and automobile care and repair. Some folks even have special rooms for sexual adventures.

Now let us consider some decisions you might make in furnishing some of your rooms.

The Living Room

In most houses this room, along with the dining room, will serve as the central focus for family gatherings for business or pleasure. This may be the hearth room in some households and therefore a center for religious activity as well and may display a household shrine or stall. If the living room serves as the main family room as well as the main room for the reception and entertainment of guests, then you may consider giving a dual personality to the room by leaving the shrine fairly inconspicuous for day to day activities, but bringing out special furnishings to redecorate the space for the purpose of holding blessings, sumbles and other ritual activities.

It is most likely that this room will be given over first to communal family activity and secondarily to the reception of guests. These two activities can be brought together insofar as many of the guests, at least the ones who frequent the household, will actually be family, or good friends who are as good as part of the family. The purpose of the living room then is to foster harmonious interaction, love and loyalty among in and to establish a sense of family identity. A deep sense of family identity is a boon to the family frith, love and good cheer. The family room, as with the ancestral shrine, is a good place for portraits of kin and mementos of ancestors, especially those who exemplified the household goals and ideals, or those noted for great deeds. If you have a family crest, display it prominently in the living room as well as over or on the ancestral shrine. If you are related to ancestors, however distant, who took part in great events in history, their portraits should be displayed prominently over your hearth or family shrine. Some members of the family should keep track of the family lore and be able to tell the tales associated with the various photos and mementos around the house. In modern times this means that you will have to study and learn your family lore in order that you may pass it on to your household. The family lore will be fairly effectively transmitted by the telling of tales and recitation of poems or even songs at sumbles, feasts, and myne-drinkings.

The atmosphere of the room should be conducive to group social interaction. This may be brought about by the use of warm color schemes and soft furniture such as couches, love seats, easy chairs or even "bean bag" chairs. You may look for furniture with soft curves and rounded edges. Of course, some may find it suits their family spirit better to have highly dynamic and energizing atmospheres created by sharp angles, cold or hot colors and exotic furnishings.

Family mottos and reminders of duty to kin and folk and so forth might be prominently displayed in a living room. One example might be the six goals displayed in a six spoked wheel. Or the nine noble virtues displayed on an eight spoked wheel with the one most cherished or characteristic of the family at the center.

Some paintings are constant reminders of the ideas they convey. Paintings of that kind serve as reminders of family ideals and identity should grace the living room walls. If paintings of the Gods and divine subjects are available to you, then you might want to include scenes of the Gods at banquets, of Goddesses such as Frigga, Idunna, Freya and other Gods and Goddesses partial to domestic affairs. Also include paintings that show different kinds of heroism or virtue meaningful to the family. Other themes of relevance to general family interests might also be included.

Dutch hex-signs are a beautiful kind of Germanic household magic. Hex-signs are a sort of "mandala" brightly painted onto a circular board or onto the house itself. These are even commercially available at very reasonable rates. Each design is given to some purpose such as health, luck, prosperity, peace, harmony, love protection, and so on. If the signs are thought of in their magical meanings on a conscious level— and then forgotten as they fade into the general æsthetic environment of the house — they will give good results. Some typical hex-sign designs are:

1

Love

2

Strength

3

Tranquility

4

Abundance

In more specialized rooms, the pictorial themes and the furnishings can be geared to facilitate particular kinds of work. If you have a place where you work on craft projects, you could hang pictures of great craftsmen, or pictures of the works you regard as great examples of craftsmanship, or images of relatives or ancestors skilled in the arts. You might also keep pictures of your own work around. An area given to a craft would benefit from dwarven presence. Appropriate subjects for art-work from the Eddas include the making of the Brising necklace, the forging of Miöllnir (Thor's hammer), Gram (the sword of Sigmund and Sigurd), Gungnir (Odin's spear). Any part of the saga of Wayland the Smith would be appropriate. Other themes might include the dwarves forging the cord that binds the Fenris-Wolf, or Dvalin and Durin forging Tyrfing (the sword of Angantyr).

You might focus on certain dwarves who made some of the same kinds of objects you work on. A jeweler might look to the dwarves who made the Brisinga-men, among whom is the dwarf, Dvalin. Any objects that help to bring the presence of the dark elves alive in the room would be welcome. If you have any tools that you use especially for holy or magical work, such as the carving of images, ritual tools or other furnishings for sanctuaries or temples, you might have them hallowed in a blessing to the dwarves or some other working in which the dwarves are called upon.

Good traditional art requires: 1) the ability to plan and design a work (measure) along with the technical skill to execute the plan, 2) the inspiration or *mania* (wode) to infuse the work with soul, and 3) it must be an imitation of some higher principle for which the art-work acts as a conduit into the world of the senses.

Used effectively, careful and conscious choices about the furnishings surrounding you and the way you arrange them can allow you to adjust or create the atmospheres and moods of your household to facilitate some kinds of activities and to discourage others.

Chapter 20
HOF AND HARROW

This chapter deals with the general principles behind the ordering of ancient holy steads and how these principles may be applied in arranging sacred sites today and tomorrow. While this information may not be of immediate use to all readers, as it pertains to the setting up of substantial physical sites, it is important to the general knowledge of the faith. Besides, those who aspire to Eldership in the Ring of Troth will want to set up a holy site of some kind for the regular practice of blessings.

The *Vé*

The *vé* [vay], the harrow and ritual itself are models of the cosmos— physical, social and psychological (or "spiritual"). Likewise the rituals that take place within the sacred enclosure are re-enactments of great "events" in the cosmic cycles or reality. Much of the symbolism of the ancient Germanic temple, ritual and art is left to be discovered or re-discovered. All of it will never be fully known, any more than all the workings of the universe symbolized in the imagery will ever be "known." Nevertheless, there is more to be said on this subject even now than easily can be pressed into a single volume.

When you are in the process of designing and building a *vé*, or when you go to the blessings at a local *vé*, and you think deeply on the meanings of the myths, the mysteries or the ordering of the *vé* will begin to rise out of the ground, the stones, and the wood-works around you and into your heart and soul.

The *vé* is basically an open air place set apart for worship. It is a place for the meeting of the folk and Gods. By establishing regular times for meeting at a specific place, both Gods and folk know where and when to meet. It is a site where the walls between Midgard and the eight worlds beyond are thinner, it is a space that partakes of both Midgard and the outer realms— it exists in heaven and on earth. In the doing of blessings, we go into the first of times— and the last of times together. We are in the "time" reflected in the "Völuspá." This is the holy time that always was and always is, the time when myths are so very real. In this time we renew ourselves and the world. Here we go to the heart of things to know our deeper selves, to come into knowledge of the parts of ourselves that are eternal and beyond the experience of our mundane egos.

Rocks, trees, groves, hills, springs or wells and grave mounds are most basic and abiding types of sites chosen for contact with the holy wights. From the 1st century to the Viking Age, outsiders consistently tell of such natural holy places among the Germanic peoples. (See *Grove and Gallows* by James A. Chisholm.)

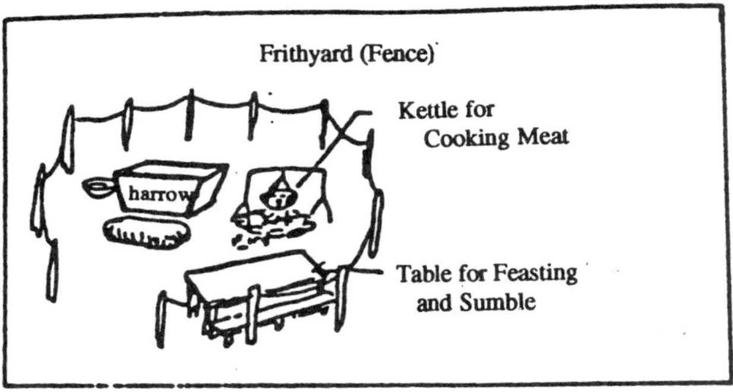

Figure 20.1: Simple *Vé* and Harrow Arrangement

The boundaries of such sites were typically marked off by a fence or wall. Such fences could consist of little more than a series of eight stakes, set in a circle, square or rectangular around the harrow or rock, tree, well, or spring and connected by twine, ropes or chains. In one instance, such a chain fence was called a "frithgarth" or "peace yard." One such pole might serve as a May-Pole in the spring celebration. If the site is a large mound or hill, the fence may be set up on the summit with a harrow at the center. We know that stakes for such yards were sometimes made of hazel, but wood from oak, yew, ash, pine or whatever wood is locally used as symbolic of Yggdrasill may be used. One advantage to the stake system is that the fence can be taken down between events if desired. Such a fence can also be portable.

If resources allow, more durable fences may be built of wood, stone, cement and other materials. Standing stones may also be set in a circle, rectangular or boat shaped configurations to mark the boundaries of the holy. Fences may also consist of hedges or trees planted near one another.

Within the yard (garth) there should be a harrow at the least. The harrow is basically an altar. It is the center of holiness, or right next to it. If a rock, tree or well is at the center, but is not shaped such that blessing bowls, mead horns and other ritual gear may be set on it, then a harrow or table may be set up beside it. The harrow may be made of a mound of stones, stones set with cement, or it may be made entirely of cement. Portable harrows, such as folding tables may also be used if necessary. These may be especially appropriate for outdoor sites that you wish to leave in a natural state most of the time.

An outdoor site should have a place for a fire. Candles do not work very well outdoors. Fire pits and outdoor grills work very well and allow you to cook in the *vé*. Small cast iron pots may sometimes be obtained for burning twigs and tinder. Other fuels that may be burned on the harrow include jelly fuels and alcohol, which may be used indoors as well as out.

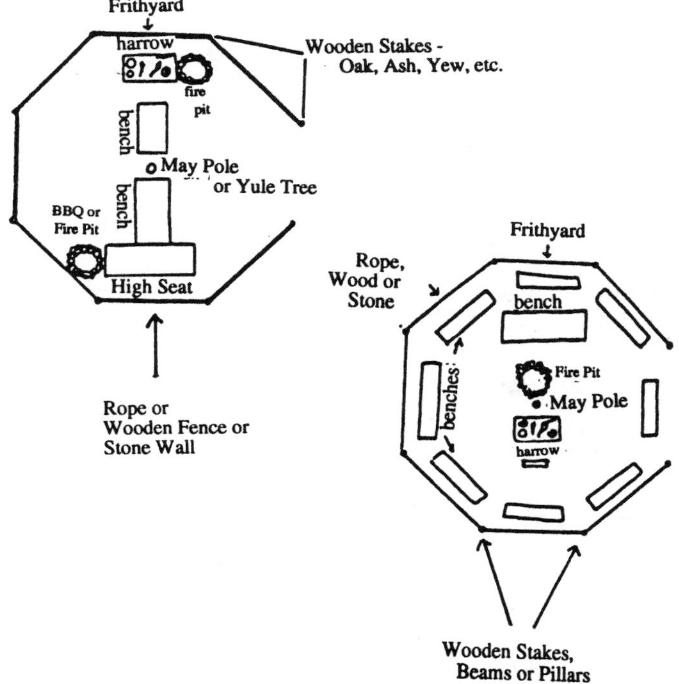

Figure 20.2: Possible Configurations of a Frithyard

The *vé* may also include benches or tables for feasting and sumble.

Another type of *vé* is the centrally planned sort which could be circular, octagonal or hexagonal and arranged about a central column with beams radiating out from the six or eight columns that support the roof, if the *vé* is to be covered. It may be left partly open and walls built between some of the columns while spaces between other columns are left open. The walls may be used to hang banners or painted with holy art and symbols. A fire and/or harrow may be placed in the south, east or north.

In outdoor settings you may also include a post to symbolize the World Tree and to function as a May-Pole for spring and summer ceremonies. Statues or carvings of Gods and heroes or other sacred symbols may be placed about the *vé* a seems most appropriate. Representations of divine personas are not necessary and some folks find them distasteful. The Roman historian Tacitus tells us that the Germans of his days did not have representations of their Gods or temples at all.

The Hof

In spite of what Tacitus says, we have numerous reports of great and splendid temples among the Germanic folk in later times. Whenever the Church moved into a Germanic region, it was faced with the task of destroying the numerous temples as well as the sacred groves, wells, and other natural sites. The ornately carved stave churches of Norway are good models for modern Hof architecture, as these beautiful designs were employed for heathen temples before they were used for churches.

The simplest form of Hof would be a basic square or rectangular building with a harrow in the center or at one end (preferably the north end). This is the shape of many of our temple buildings will likely take in the earlier years of our development, since the arrangement can be formed from a single room in a house, garage, or property leased for the purpose. Ideally, there will be a place for fire, such as a fireplace, a wood burning or coal burning stove, an electric or gas stove, or at least a place for candles or a bowl of alcohol or some jelly fuel. In Viking Age temples and halls the fires were typically in the middle of the floor though it is now more practical for hearths and other sacred furniture to be positioned against a wall.

One very traditional way to set up such holy halls is to position along one wall a table that is slightly raised on a platform about a foot or a foot and a half in height. Two rows of benches may then be set perpendicular to the high-seat table. Two columns may be set to either side of the high-seat. In ancient halls long fire pits ran the length of the building in the center of the hall. Though this is generally impractical now, candles or lanterns may be set on tables as a substitute. The sumble horn is passed over these fires when it is hallowed.

Some Viking Age hofs had a room adjoining the main hall. It was in this smaller room that the sacrificial animals were slaughtered and the blessing feast was prepared— it was something like a sacred kitchen. In modern household situations the kitchen/dining room arrangement generally fits this ancient model. In buildings built to be public hofs there should be kitchen facilities for feasts. To either side of the fires, nearly against the rows of benches, there were typically a row of columns running down the room from the high-seat pillars. Enough room should be left between the fires and the benches to allow for processions and dances around the room. According to the *Eyrbryggja Saga* the pillars to the entrance of a temple of Thor were studded with "regin nails" or "godly nails." If the pillars were carved, and an image of Thor was included it is possible that these nails might serve to symbolize the whetstone that was lodged in Thor's head during his fight with the giant named Hrungnir.

For indoor sites, especially those which are used for daily activities most of the time, you might make a folding three panel screen to set up in front of the harrow. Such a screen could be painted or otherwise decorated with holy symbols. If the hof has a symbol of its own, this symbol should take a central place. Likewise, if the hof is given to the worship of a particular deity, then an image particular to that deity ought to have a central place as well. Representational images of the Gods and Goddesses, such as pillars carved with the likenesses of the deities might be included, though they are certainly not necessary. If it is for a private Hearth level, harrow images and tokens of kinsmen past might be included.

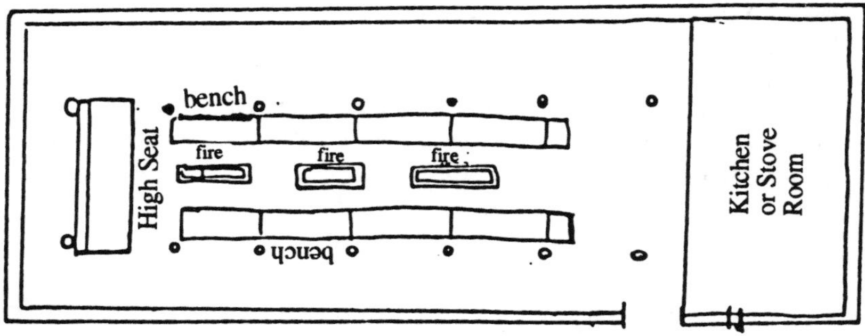

Figure 20.3: Typical Hof Plan

Harrow Furnishings

For blessings, a harrow should have fire on or near it and a liquid, such as mead, ale or apple juice. This liquid should begin the blessing in a bottle or jug to be poured later into a horn or bowl from which it is given to the gathered folk. There should then be a blessing bowl into which the remainder is poured from the horn. The liquid is then poured from the blessing bowl out onto the earth or into an auxiliary bowl on the floor indoors— and later poured onto the earth after the blessing is ended.

A lot-tine, which takes the shape of a sprig of evergreen should be on the harrow for sprinkling the blessings from the blessing bowl upon the harrow and folk. Other items might include an oath-ring (large enough for the wrist or arm), a hammer, or a wand might be included for hallowing purposes. The ring is on the harrow for the swearing of oaths. All sorts of other things might also be placed upon the harrow according to individual preferences.

In the blessings of the days of yore fire was used to cook or boil the food that was to be hallowed for the feast. Nowadays the fires are usually small and placed on the harrow itself, though the use of large cooking fires is not unknown. When a sumble horn is filled or refilled, it is customary to pass it over the fire and sign it with the hammer mark to hallow it.

Small fires to be set atop harrows may be best placed in iron or earthenware fire pots. It is possible to use twigs and herbs for indoor fires, though it is advisable to experiment with the available woods to see which burn most cleanly. Jelly fuel and rubbing alcohol may be used as well. These burn clean and cool. Candles and incense may also serve as fire at indoor blessings.

Ovens, hearths, and wood burning stoves may also serve as sacred fires for indoor rites. The pilot light of a gas stove may be regarded as the equivalent of an eternal hearth flame.

Outdoor fires may be set in fire pits and outdoor grills for cooking sacrificial meals. Over pits you may set a spit for roasting meat or hanging kettles.

These general guidelines are based on literary and archaeological evidence from the first century through the Viking Age. Certain innovations, such as the use of some jelly fuel or alcohol for harrow fires are made for the sake of practicality in the modern world. Innovation is heartily encouraged as is drawing inspiration from ancient models.

Part III
Ring of Troth

Chapter 21
THE ROLE OF ELDERS

The Troth has no popes, no dogmas and no heresies. Elders, or "priests" are not responsible, as it is with some faiths, to provide a link between the worlds of the divine and the mundane realm. It is not the place of Elders to tell true folk how to think about the Gods and Goddesses. It is expected that in a room with three different true folk there will be four different opinions on theological matters. The fourth opinion is sometimes a harmonious combination of the first three. Being human, many are even liable to believe that everybody who holds a different opinion is all wrong-headed and should desist from spreading their error-filled ideas.

If there were an official pronouncement by the Eldership on matters of theology, it would be that all are entitled to hold their own beliefs and to worship in their own manner. If a person declares that he or she is true to the elder Gods and religious ways of the northern tribes, then that person is true as far as the Eldership is concerned. Troth is based on understanding, and everybody has a slightly different experiential and conceptual basis from which to assess their experiences and, hence each arrives at a slightly different conclusion regarding the nature of divinity and the meaning and uses of myth and ritual.

Furthermore, the interceding of Elders is not required for one to have knowledge or experience of the holy as priests are required in the Catholic Church for contact with the sacred and the Christian God. Elders specialize in calling on the Gods for group celebrations, but their presence is not required.

You might then ask why we have Elders at all if we value freedom of belief and worship so dearly. There are several reasons why *trained* Elders are important at this point in the (re-)development of the Troth. The first is that our religion is a folk religion whose continuity was seriously disrupted by forced conversions and methodical suppression. The attempted suppression of the Troth is still going on today— now Church officials still attempt to take away our "Christmas trees" and Easter bunnies— seeing them for what they are: *survivals of the heathen heritage*. But fortunately Church dogmatists no longer command the power of the state in enforcing their doctrines. Besides they would meet with little more success than their predecessors who have tried to stamp out such survivals for centuries.

But because of the total disruption in our own lore few of our folk have been raised in the Troth and all must learn about the traditions anew from academic research and personal experience and experimentation. Most folks do not have the time or inclination to learn how to read the old languages in which our primary sources exist, or even to plough through all the material in modern English and synthesize it for practical use. Most folks would rather have access to someone who has deep knowledge of the lore and who has extensive experience in applying it to get answers to basic questions about the religion, the myths and their relevance to daily life in Midgard, than take several years out of their own lives to go through the process themselves. Right now we are at a stage where practically everybody who sincerely wants to practice the way of the Troth has to study hard just to get the basics, and harder still to get at deeper meanings of the myths and rituals, or even to reconstruct the rituals.

When Elders are numerous, and people with the knowledge of the founding Elders are commonplace, the rudiments can be more readily acquired as the raw material has been made practical. Thus basic knowledge once more will become easily available by word of mouth— just as it was in olden times. But nowadays, many people want answers to questions about the lore that they do not feel equipped to handle themselves due to their lack of training in language, history, literature, mythology or practical experience of the faith. They would gladly seek the advice of someone they *trusted* and who had this experience. Some people have a difficult time making the Troth "work" for them at first. Here again access to an experienced Elder certainly would be welcomed.

It is through a number of people with a thorough knowledge of the authentic older tradition that the Troth will again reach the stage where it is an oral tradition learned simply by being a part of the culture. In these initial stages, however, we need to be sure that the people who have the most thorough understanding of the old religion and ways are the ones who are most active in helping others to understand and practice the religion today. Once the stage has been reached where the Troth is again a religion of the folk and religious education is again in the hands of the family and local community, then we will no longer be in such great need of Elders to act as educators.

When the Troth is again a folk religion in fact as well as in theory, Elders will be responsible for maintaining houses of public worship and for administering public blessings, especially the great seasonal blessings.

In the meantime, in our struggles to practice the religion authentically, we respect the knowledge and opinions of those who dedicate their lives to recovering the older Troth. In *Idunna* and other Troth publications, you will find a variety of opinions. The rede of most individuals may be regarded as simply opinion. An Elder acts as an official representative of the Troth and has the power to make official pronouncements on theology— but only insofar as to say: "This is the most traditional way of looking at this question." These opinions will not be doctrine and no one will be required to believe them— but they will become a matter of public record. In fact, the rede of two Elders may sometimes be at variance, especially if one Elder is dedicated to the path of, let's say, Tyr, and the other to the way of Frey, for example. Taking different spiritual paths will result in different perspectives on things. The Elder will have the authority to declare ideas and interpretations of the lore as traditional or authentic. When you read the opinion of an Elder, you can *trust* that you have read the opinion of someone who has dedicated a significant portion of his or her life to finding out just what the tradition is, and to living it in the modern world.

Chapter 22
STARTING HEARTHS

Anyone can start a kindred in the Troth. All you need to do is get together with another true person and start calling yourself a kindred and start performing the blessings of the year according to some Germanic tradition. You are then true and have a true kindred.

However, if you and the others involved in your kindred would like to become officially affiliated with the Ring of Troth, you may make an application for changing your kindred over into a Hearth. This is essentially a small group of individual practitioners of the Troth who are bound together in trust and fellowship to follow the true ways of their ancestors of the north.

If you feel yourself to be a lone practitioner of the Troth— alone in a sea of people who just don't seem to understand your religious longings, take heart. Once back in the early 1980s there was a young man handing out religious tracts imploring his fellow students at the University of Texas to return to the religion of Thor. When he was approached and told of the whole Ásatrú movement he was shocked— he thought that surely no one else could have thought the way he did!

To start a kindred or Hearth just begin asking around, put up notices at bookstores, put ads in newspapers. Once you get a core group, the rest will be easy. But you have to get the word out to the public in your own area that in fact there are fellow Trothers in the vicinity. The Ring of Troth may also be able to put you in touch with other potential Hearth members if you are yourself an official member of the Ring.

Once you have your group founded, the main purpose of the meetings should focus on the performance of the blessings and the learning of the lore. *A Book of Troth* should perhaps be studied in conjunction with the *Poetic* and *Prose Eddas* and a good general introduction to the mythology (such as the ones by Ellis Davidson or Turville-Petre). Lore and the learning of lore is always important, but it is always secondary to practice. The lore can only be understood fully once there has been a significant amount of practice of the blessings and rites. It is sometimes helpful to remember that in ancient times our ancestors would have experienced thousands of rites and customs in a direct and sensual way before reaching a state of intellectual and spiritual maturity sufficient to absorb the lore of the myths in a meaningful way.

Try to keep Hearth and kindred gatherings focused on *doing* rather than thinking. Any time a Trother goes to a gathering he or she should go away having had a good time with good company. In days of yore religious gatherings were also opportunities for "entertainment." For in those days it was sometimes impossible to distinguish between what we call religion and entertainment today. In that regard, Jim and Tammy weren't that far off the mark. Except in this Wolf-Age, entertainment has become a religion where rock stars and sports "heroes" are the new gods. These would seem to be poor substitutes for the real things, however.

Leadership of the kindred or Hearth should be decided in any way the members see fit. But there should be a designated leadership role as well as some sort of name for the kindred. This helps give direction and identity to the group— both factors which will weigh heavily in its future chances of success.

Appendix A
Brewing Mead

We can tell you how to make mead, but we cannot tell you how to make a consistent quality of mead. The outer quality of the mead has much to do with the spiritual circumstances surrounding its fermentation. Besides, in the context of a sumble all mead tastes good— even the muddy dregs from the bottom of the jug.

The basic ingredients for mead include honey, water and yeast. Some brewers use only the basics. Most have more complex formulas— some made with cranberries and beer ingredients. Archaeological evidence shows that Viking Age meads were beer-meads with several kinds of berries thrown in. Beers seem to have been made with berries as well.

This recipe is designed for a five gallon batch. To make smaller batches, reduce the ingredients proportionately. Big batches cost a lot and can be a big waste on those rare occasions when they go completely foul. But if they turn out well you can afford to be very generous with it. If you make a one gallon batch you have got hardly enough for a sumble. One gallon batches are good for testing daring new recipes and that is about it. A five gallon batch will get a small Hearth through several blessings and perhaps two or three sumbles.

Basic Dry Mead

10-15 lbs. honey
Use pure raw honey rather than pasteurized honey if possible.

5 gallons of spring or pure water
Some well washed lemon peels or 10-15 tsp. of mallic acid.
4-6 tsp. of strong tea or 7-8 tsp. of tartaric acid
5 tsp. yeast energizer or yeast nutrient
1-2 packets of Champagne or mead yeast

Mead Making Tools

1. Get a big kettle that will hold 3-5 gallons. It should be very clean. The smoother the better. Enamel coated pans clean better than aluminum because they are smoother. An aluminum pan will retain the flavors of anything else it holds and is likely to impart this to your mead. Enamel can be cleaned of most flavors of things previously cooked in pots coated with it.
2. A big bucket or crock that can hold 7-8 gallons. Sometimes you can find 7 1/2 gallon buckets made especially for the purpose of brewing. These include a lid and an airlock.
3. A five gallon water jar with a narrow neck and several smaller bottles.
4. Several air locks. These are sold wherever wine and beer making supplies are sold.

5. Save up a large number of wine and beer bottles and get corks and rubber stoppers with holes for air locks. Make sure that the corks and stoppers fit your bottles. You will need to air lock about 2 gallons, but you will need bottles and corks for about 7 gallons.

Procedures

Warm up over half the water in the pan and mix in the honey and all the other ingredients except the yeast. Stir it and heat it until it is about to boil, then dump it into the plastic bucket or crock. Then heat up the rest of the water and add it to the bucket. Do not boil your mead or else the good brewers will make fun of you. They will shake their heads and say: "Boiled mead!" Let the liquid in the bucket cool for a day and then add the yeast as directed by the instructions on the back of the yeast packet. Keep it at room temperature— look at the yeast packet for ideal temperature ranges. Put an air lock on the lid. In a day or two it will be fermenting. It will continue to ferment for several days after which it will slow down. Please note: The air lock should have some water in it. Its function is to allow the gasses produced as a result of the fermentation process to escape while preventing bacteria floating in the air from getting into the must.

When the fermentation slows down it is going into the secondary fermentation stage. At this point it should be siphoned out of the bucket and into the 5 gallon jar and other bottles. These bottles should have air locks. Be sure to leave the muddy sediment at the bottom of the bottle. Secondary fermentation may go on for several months, after which the mead may be siphoned off into the wine and beer bottles from which it will be dispensed at a feast or sumble.

Those who are patient and particular may want to siphon their mead a second time after several months in order to ensure its clarity. Transferring mead from one bottle to another is known in brewing jargon as "racking." For best results you should store your mead in the dark at room temperature. Be sure to cork the bottles. If the mead is not really finished fermenting, the corks may pop out, or the bottle will pop and emit gas when you open it.

Always keep your equipment clean. Sterilize all your tools before you use it. Rinse it well so that none of your soap or bleach or sodium bisulfate gets in your brew. In medieval France the death penalty was administered to sloppy brewers.

If all this seems like it would be fun, then incorporate it into the running of your true household. If it seems to be a lot of bother, then buy Merrydown or some other commercial mead, ale or apple juice.

Please note: Mead tends to be rather strong in comparison with all that thin beer we are used to here in the States. Mead is actually a honey-wine, and has an average of 12% alcohol.

Appendix B
Booklist

Bauschatz, Paul C. *The Well and the Tree: World and Time in Early Germanic Culture*. Amherst: University of Massachusetts Press, 1982. [Definitive introduction to basic principles of Germanic cosmology beginning with time and space.]

Bord, Janet and Colin. *Sacred Waters: Holy Wells and Water Lore in Britain and Ireland*. London: Granada, 1985.

Chambers, E. K. *The Medieval Stage*. London: Oxford University Press, 1903, 2 vols.
[An excellent discussion of the continuation of heathen dance, drama and other festive activity into the Christian Middle Ages. It contains an in-depth treatment of seasonal customs and festive activities.]

Chisholm, James Allen. *Grove and Gallows*. (Unpublished MS).
[A collection of many of the references to Germanic religion contained in the works of a ancient Greek and Latin authors.]

———————————. *EDDA: Keys to the Northern Mysteries*. (Unpublished MS).
[This is a translation of the *Elder* or *Poetic Edda* designed to give the reader maximum insight into the mind of the poets and into the culture that produced the text. Much of the technical religious terminology that cannot be translated accurately by any modern equivalent is retained in the translation and explained in notes and glossary.]

Davidson, Hilda R. (Ellis). *The Road to Hel*. Cambridge: Cambridge University Press, 1943.
[An insightful discussion of Germanic burial practices and ways of thinking about the worlds beyond Midgard.]

———————. *Gods and Myths of Northern Europe*. Harmondsworth: Penguin, 1964.
[This is one of the best and most widely available introductions to Germanic religion in English.]

Dumézil, Georges. *The Destiny of a Warrior*. tr. A. Hiltebeitel. Chicago: University of Chicago Press, 1970.

——————. *From Myth to Fiction: The Saga of Hadingus*. tr. D. Coltman. Chicago: University of Chicago Press, 1973.
[By showing structural similarities between some of the myths of the Vanic Gods, especially Niord, and some of the stories of Hadingus, Dumézil offers insights into the nature of the Vanir.]

——————. *Gods of the Ancient Northmen*. E. Haugen, ed. Berkeley: University of California Press, 1973.
[This contains Dumézil's ground breaking thesis on the Indo-European trifunctional social model as it applies to the Germanic pantheon.]

Finch, R. G. *The Saga of the Volsungs*. London: Nelson, 1965.
[This is the material from which Wagner's *Ring* cycle is ultimately derived. There is so much to be gained concerning religion and ethics from this saga that it is impossible to summarize it all here. This is the*whole* story of Sigurd, the Dragon-Slayer.]

Gaster, Theodor H. *The New Golden Bough: A New Abridgement of the Classic Work by James Frazer*. New York: S. G. Phillips, 1959.
[This is not merely an abridgement, but also a revision. Much of the material has been updated. The book contains numerous accounts of European seasonal and household customs of heathen derivation.]

Gomme, George L. *British Folk-lore*. London: National Homereading Union, 1916.
[An impressive collection of British folklore, games and customs.]

Grimm, Jacob. *Teutonic Mythology*. tr. S. Stallybrass. New York: Dover, 1966, 4 vols.
[This is a treasure house of heathen Germanic lore. It is sprinkled with untranslated quotes from the primary sources in their original languages. Though many of Grimm's conclusions may be dated (the work was originally published in the early 1800s) his observations are insightful.]

Grønbech, Vilhelm. *The Culture of the Teutons*. London: Oxford University Press, 1931, 2 vols.
[This work is essential to understanding the Germanic soul concepts such as *hamingja* (haming) and how they are integrally woven into the fabric of everyday life in values, ethics and ideals and actual practice.]

Gurevich, Aron. *Medieval Popular Culture: Problems of Belief and Perception*. Cambridge: Cambridge University Press, 1988.
[This contains a fine discussion of the persistence of heathenism as revealed by Church penitentials.]

Hollander, Lee M., tr. *The Poetic Edda*. Austin: University of Texas Press, 1962, 2nd ed.
[The *Poetic Edda* is the primary source for Viking Age myth and religion. This work dense and a single stanza can bear the weight of many meanings. Multiple levels of meaning cannot be conveyed effectively in translation since much relies on apparent word-play. Hollander's translation captures the beauty of the original poetry by using original meters and by using Germanic English vocabulary. This makes for a sometimes difficult style to understand at first. Hollander also often strays from literal translation and no effort has been made to preserve original religious terminology.]

Jones, Gwyn. *A History of the Vikings*. London: Oxford University Press, 1984, 2nd ed.
[This is *the* definitive history of the Vikings. It is a bit dense and heavy going for the casual reader.]

Jones, Gwyn, tr. *Erik the Red and other Icelandic Sagas*. Oxford: Oxford University Press, 1961.
[This contains an English translation of *Hrolf Kraki's Saga* as well as several family sagas.]

Kelcher, Georgia Dunham. *Dreams in Old Norse Literature and their Affinities in Folklore*. Cambridge: Cambridge University Press, 1935.
[Here is a detailed study of types of dreams found in Old Norse sources. Original Old Norse text along with translations are included.]

Knightly, Charles. *The Customs and Ceremonies of Britain: An Encyclopaedia of Living Traditions with a Calendar of Customs and a Regional Gazetter*. London: Thames and Hudson, 1986.
[This contains brief accounts of hundreds of ancient and living customs with discussions of their origins and details of their practice. This includes charts showing when and where the customs are practiced.]

Pálsson, Hermann and Edwards, Paul, tr. and ed. *Seven Viking Romances*. Harmondsworth: Penguin, 1985.
[This is a collection of "sagas of ancient times." These are distinguished from the "family sagas" in that they are rooted more in myth than in history. This kind of saga supplements the myths, while the family sagas give insight into daily life and the practice of religion and ethics in heathen Iceland.]

Philpotts, Bertha. *The Elder Edda and Ancient Scandinavian Drama*. Cambridge: Cambridge University Press, 1920.

Porter, E. *The Folklore of East Anglia*. London: Batsford, 1974.

Simpson, J. *The Folklore of Sussex*. London: Batsford, 1973.

—————. *Everyday Life in the Viking Age*. New York: Dorset Press, 1967.

Sturluson, Snorri. *Edda*. tr. Anthony Faulkes. Rutland, VT: Tuttle, 1987.
[This is the most complete translation of the *Prose Edda* currently widely available in English. It even includes the usually omitted Háttatal section. Snorri's work is essential to understanding the ancient Scandinavian mythology.]

Thorsson, Edred. *A Book of Troth*. St. Paul, MN: Llewellyn, 1989.
[The original definitive book on the practice of the older Troth in today's world, and the first official basic manual of the Ring of Troth.]

Turville-Petre, E.O.G. *Myth and Religion of the North*. New York: Holt, Rinehart and Winston, 1964.
[This is the best general introduction to Germanic religion in English.]

Vries, Jan de. *Altgermanische Religionsgeschichte*. Berlin: de Gruyter, 1956-57, 2 vols.
[This is absolutely the best and most complete overview of Germanic religion available in any language. The text is in German.]

Vries, Jan de. *Altnordisches etymologisches Wörterbuch*. Leiden: Brill, 1961. [This German language etymological dictionary of Old Norse is indispensable for the study of the lore from the original Old Norse sources.]

Williams, Mary. *Social Scandinavia in the Viking Age*. New York: MacMillan, 1930.
[This book presents a good overview of the material and social life of Scandinavia at the end of the heathen period.]

Appendix C

Glossary

Æsir, sg. *Áss*: The Gods and Goddesses of consciousness in the Germanic pantheon, governing the powers of sovereignty and physical force.

ætt, pl. *ættir*: Family or genus, used as a name for the threefold divisions of the futhark and eight divisions of the heavens. Also means a group or division of eight.

Asgard: The enclosure of the Gods, the realm where the Gods and Goddesses exist. (ON *Ásgarðr*)

bind-rune: Two or more runestaves superimposed over one another, sometimes used to form galdor-staves.

blessing: The act of sacrificing and distributing the power of the Gods and Goddesses in Midgard. (OE *blôtan* and *bletsian*, to sacrifice)

boast: A ritual drinking to the honor of a God, Goddess, or ancestor, or drinking to seal an oath for future actions. Also a "toast." (OE *bêot*)

call: The part of a ritual in which the divine forces to take part in the blessing are invoked.

dis, pl. dises: Ancestral female divinities to whom Winter Nights and Disting are holy. (ON *dís*; *dísir*)

drinking: The part of a ritual in which the liquid charged with the divine forces is ingested by the gathered folk.

earth: 1) The natural, physical aspects of the universe, 2) The planet Earth, 3) soil.

etin: A "giant," which is a living entity of great age, strength, and often knowledge. (ON sg. *jötunn*; pl. *jötnar*)

fetch: A numinous being attached to every individual, which is the repository of all past action and which accordingly affects the person's life: the personal divinity.

folk: 1) The Teutonic or Germanic nation (all people of Teutonic heritage, German, English, Dutch, Scandinavian, etc.), 2) The people gathered for a holy event.

frith: The true Germanic word for "peace" which carries with it the implication of "freedom."

galdor: 1) A magical incantation or mantra. 2) A form of magic which often uses runestaves as a method of objectifying verbal contents and thus objectify magical intent. (ON *galdr*, pl. *galdrar*)

gand: The magical wand. (ON *gandr*)

giving: The part of a ritual in which the remainder of the charged liquid not consumed by the gathered folk is returned to the divine realm. Also called the"yielding."

grith: Another word for "peace" which carries the implication of "security."

hallowing: The part of a ritual in which the space where the ritual is to be performed is marked off from the profane world, made holy, and protected.

haming: Derived from ON *hamingja*: Mobile magical force rather like the *mana* of other traditions. Often defined as "luck," "shape-shifting force," or "guardian spirit."
harrow: 1) An outdoor altar usually made of stone, 2) A general term of the altar in a true working. (OE *hearg*)
holy: There are two aspects to this term: 1) that which is filled with divine power, and 2) that which is marked off and separate from the profane.
howe: A grave. Often in the form of a burial mound built over a pit.
hidge: The cognitive part of the soul, the intellect or "mind." Also called hugh. (OE *hyge*)
hyde: The quasi-physical part of the soul which gives a person shape and form. (ON *hamr*)
leaving: The formal closing of a ritual.
loading: The part of a ritual in which the sacred power that has been called upon is channeled into the holy drink.
lore: The tradition in all its aspects.
lyke: The physical part of the soul-body (psycho-physical) complex. Also called lich. (OE *lîc*)
Midgard: the dwelling place of humanity, the physical plane of existence. Also, Mid-yard, the enclosure in the midst of all. (OE *Middangeard*) Meddlert.
might: Not only physical power but also spiritual force.
mood: The emotional part of the soul closely allied with the wode. (OE *môd*)
multiverse: The many states of being (worlds) that make up the universe. Used when focusing on the multiplicity of being.
myne: The reflective part of the soul, the memory: personal and transpersonal. (OE *mynd*; ON *minni*)
nine noble virtues: A set of ethical precepts in the modern Troth. They are: 1) courage, 2) truth, 3) honor, 4) fidelity, 5) discipline, 6) hospitality, 7) industriousness, 8) self-reliance, and 9) perseverance.
norn: One of the three female wights who embody the process of casue and effect and evolutionary force.
ørlög: ON Literally analyzed this means "primal layers" (primal laws)— the past action of an individual or the cosmos) that shapes present reality, and that which should come about as a result of it. Its root concept is the same as English wyrd or weird.
ragnarök: ON Literally this means the "judgment of the Gods," it is an end of a cycle of existence.
reading: The part of a ritual in which a mythic-poetic text is recited in order to place the gathering into a mythic time/space, to engage in the mythic flow of timelessness.
rede: The part of a ritual in which the purpose of the working is stated.
seith: A kind of magical technique contrasted with galdor. Seith involves attaining of trance states and often involves sexuality. Sometimes this

involves shape-shifting into animal forms. Typically it is performed by volvas who would roam the countryside and attend feasts where they would sit on a wooden platform amd with the aid of the magical songs of their assistants they could obtain visions of the future. It is the kind of magic taught to Odin by Freya.

six-fold goal: A set of ethical aims of behavior in the modern Troth. They are 1) right (justice), 2) wisdom (intelligence), 3) might (strength), 4) harvest (prosperity), 5) frith (peace), and 6) love (pleasure).

soul: 1) A general term for the psychic parts of the psycho-physical complex, 2) The postmortem shade. (OE *sawl*)

stall: An indoor altar.

stave: A spell or a rune.

sumble: The sacred ritual feast at which boasts are drunk.(OE *symble*)

thurs: A strong kind of giant devoid of intelligence.

tide: A time, occasion, a span of time with a definite beginning and end. Example: Yule-tide.

tine: A talisman.

troth: Religion, being loyal to the Gods and Goddesses and cultural values of the ancestors. (ON *trú*, OE *trêowþ*)

true: Adjectival form of "troth," can mean "loyal." A "true man" is a man loyal to the Gods and Goddesses of his ancestors.

Vanir, sg. Van: ON The Gods and Goddesses of organic existence in the Germanic pantheon, governing the realms of organic production, eroticism, wealth, craftsmanship, and physical well-being.

vé ON An outdoor sacred enclosure open to the sky.

volva: A female magician who specializes in seith magic.

wight: A being or entity of any kind with some living quality.

worship: Literally this means simply "to give honor (worth) to something— and that is all that it means in the terminology of the Troth.

wode: An emotive, synthesizing part of the soul which brings various aspects together in a powerful and inspired way. Related to the mood. (OE *wôd*, ON *óðr*)

world: The "psycho-chronic" human aspects of the manifested universe. (OE *weoruld*, the age of a man.) The cosmos.

World-Tree, see Yggdrasill.

wyrd: The process of the unseen web of synchronicity and cause and effect throughout the cosmos. Same as weird.

Yggdrasill: The framework of the cosmos which supports the nine major realms or worlds.

About the Author

James Allen Chisholm was the first Steersman of the Ring of Troth, an office he assumed on Mother Night (December 20), 1987ce. He relinquished that title and sacred office at Ostara 1992. The present work was completed during his tenure as Steersman. He has since pursued varied interests in scholarship and metallurgy. James holds a Master of Arts in History from the University of Texas at Austin and has taught Art History at the college level. He presently lives in Houston, Texas.